NEITHER CREATED NOR DESTROYED

Josh,

Thank you <u>so</u> much for your support. It is really cool to have read your story and share mine with you now. I quite literally couldn't have done this without you! Sending you all the light and magic.

your pal,

Nicki

5/27/21

NEITHER CREATED NOR DESTROYED

A Memoir

Nicki Avena

NEW DEGREE PRESS

NEITHER CREATED NOR DESTROYED

A Memoir

ISBN

978-1-63676-841-0 *Paperback*

978-1-63730-201-9 *Kindle Ebook*

978-1-63730-285-9 *Digital Ebook*

For Jenny, to whom I'll always be a ninny.

CONTENTS

I will never have
this version of me again
let me slow down
and be with her

—ALWAYS EVOLVING, RUPI KAUR

AUTHOR'S NOTE

A year after the sudden death of my older sister, I found myself traveling through Europe. At 1:00 a.m. I laid on my Airbnb mattress in the dark. The bedframe was so low to the ground I was practically on the floor. I held my phone up to my face, squinting into the blinding screen. My schedule allowed one remaining day in Paris, already stacked with activities, but something nagged me to see an opera before leaving. A strange craving, as I'd never seen an opera before. I scrolled the website of the renowned Parisian opera house, the Palais Garnier, for available opera tickets. There were none for tomorrow night, but there were some for a contemporary dance. *Good enough* I thought, barely skimming the description. I clicked "add to cart," squirmed in tangles of bed sheets, and reached over the mattress's edge for my wallet.

The following evening there were four acts. The first two were highly abstracted. I was grateful for intermission, when I downed two fizzing glasses of pink wine while overlooking a grand, marble foyer. By the fourth act my buzz was sound. Through rosé glossed eyes I observed a pink flock of ballerinas tiptoeing to and fro. One dancer was pulled away by a dark, hooded figure who held her by the wrist. The tempo quickened and she twirled faster and faster, leaping violently around the stage. A hierarchy clarified. The figure controlled her like a single, omnipotent God. I was watching the renown 1913 ballet *The Rite of Spring* by Igor Stravinsky. The choreography represented a girl in Pagan Russia chosen as a human sacrifice. She danced herself to death to propitiate the god of spring.

Like a Rorschach test, I projected onto her. I saw myself reflected in her Herculean leaps, pirouetting, and dipping around the influences of my successive traumas. Including a tumultuous childhood, innumerable heartbreaks, the death of a sibling, and the complicated quest to womanhood, I saw how hastily these caused me to move around my life. Watching her, watching *myself*, I too felt exhausted, pining for respite.

A millennial woman in her early thirties, my story begins in 1989. It is one about my body, my family, trauma, grief, healing, the dichotomy of "right" and "wrong," and the lifelong search for *belonging*. I felt called to weave my memories into one story because writing invariably helps me see more clearly. It deepens my connection to myself and my purpose in this life. I aspire to filter my lived experiences into a great pool of meaning.

As there is wisdom in contextualizing ourselves within society at large, I struggle to validate my losses and gains. However, only in taking accountability for our individual and nuanced parts in what we have survived are we able to authentically engage with the world around us, contributing more effectively to the whole.

Through living and writing this book, I have learned that hardships are less terminal endings than they are critical transitions. The Latin etymology of the word *victim* is victima and means "sacrificial animal; person or animal killed as a sacrifice."[1] Like in *The Rite of Spring*, my memoir asks how our sacrifices prime us for deeper understandings of the human condition. Losses and mistakes produce fertile soil for empathy, integrity, and expansion.

The names of the individuals in this book have been altered or omitted to respect privacy. Some people or events were withheld, where appropriate, to sharpen the overarching message of each chapter.

You may like this book if you enjoy a commixture of fact and feeling. You may like this book if you appreciate stories on overcoming adversity. You may like this book if you're unafraid of facing difficult truths. You may like this book if you believe that magic is real. You may like this book if you're willing to investigate your own humanity, and if you're not afraid to show your ass. You may especially like this book if you've made a covenant to live your life bravely and with heart.

---

1 *Online Etymology Dictionary,* Douglas Harper, 2001–2021, Accessed January 29, 2021.

PART ONE

1

MIRACLES AND MISTAKES

I was born surviving.

In late December of 1989, two delivery room nurses placed their hands on the obliques of my pregnant mother, who laid moaning in her hospital bed. They rolled and rocked her from side to side, trying to unravel the umbilical cord wrapping itself around my neck, panicking as my oxygen levels decreased. The doctor was called in to perform an emergency Cesarean section. A slit here, an incision there, and I was hand plucked from the womb like a ripened fig. (Phew!) I made it. Legend has it I was enormous.

• • •

Five years earlier, in 1984, my grandparents on my mother's side were the first to leave. They abandoned their substantial New York legacy and, hailing all the way from Long Island, permanently relocated to Florida, settling in the small, East Coast city of Ormond Beach.

As spring break surged and Ormond Beach attracted national attention, real estate developments marketed cheap land and easy living countrywide, especially to Northeasterners subjected to the city grind. *And Lo!* My parents were next. Drawn from the north to the south by the combination of these charms, in 1987, they followed my grandparent's lead. They purchased a plot of land far from the center of town, in a brand-new neighborhood, mostly undomesticated wilderness. In its clearings they laid the bedrock for what I would come to know as *home.*

Despite its natural beauty, their new town invited heathenry, summoning seasonal migrations of biblical proportions. Tourists descended like locust swarms upon a petite field of crops. Once a year, attendance rose from its usual sixty thousand residents to three hundred and fifty thousand visitors.[2] However lawless, the tourism injected more than $120 million into the local economy each season.[3] There were catalytic sponsorships of the event all along the beachside by Marlboro, Miller, and MTV.

MTV, video jockeys, pray for us sinners, now and at the hour of our death, Amen.

As they established themselves, my mom and dad formed new friendships in the community, including a couple in their neighborhood who was expecting a child. The couple frequently complained there weren't any retailers in the area who sold items for babies. My parents needed jobs and, inspired by the economic flourish, they noted the gap in the marketplace, obtained a business license, and opened a small store in town selling baby furniture.

---

2 "The History of Spring Break Travel: A Retrospective," *On Call International* (blog), March 7, 2013, accessed January 8, 2021.

3 Chris Graham, "Daytona Beach Not the Spring Break Hot Spot It Once Was," *The Daytona Beach News-Journal,* March 23, 2013.

Part of the impetus for opening the store was that my parents wanted to have a child of their own, but my mother was soon after diagnosed with a condition rendering her unable to become pregnant. My dad has since boasted about flying my mother to medical professionals all across America. My mother recalls seeing one doctor in Georgia, a stone's throw over the state line.

They sought reproductive alternatives. In 1988, they adopted a daughter. They named her Allie.

Three months after the adoption, much to her surprise, my mother received a belated RSVP. Not on ornate stationary, but via pregnancy test, she discovered she was expectant with me.

Once, when I was twenty-seven years old, I sat in the audience of a comedy club in a dark, brick-lined basement in Washington DC. The comic on stage started a joke about being a "miracle baby," which is what my mom has always called me. I perked up. However, the punchline of the joke was that he'd not realized until adulthood that the word "miracle" was easily interchangeable with the word "mistake."

A mistake? Flummoxed, I chewed on this joke for a week. *What does it mean to arrive to this world unplanned?* I asked myself. I was once a miracle, now a vagabond, rogue and unbelonging. Eventually, I mustered the courage to ask my mom the truth through the boundary of a telephone. How did she feel discovering she was pregnant with a second kid?

Her voice was delicate and encouraging. "Of course, I was grateful," she said. I exhaled. "I was surprised," she continued, "but I felt like I had been blessed." She was happy Allie would walk through life with a companion. Allie, however, was pissed. Laughing, she described how Allie scaled the walls of my crib at night. With a Sumo wrestler's dexterity, she flipped over the sides, soared into the crib, and belly flopped onto my body, proving her dominance as the eldest sibling—an impassioned greeting.

A couple years after I was born, the economy of my parents' relationship, and also of the town, became unviable. In 1993, my parents divorced. My mother found a new job with the Postal Service, routing mail trucks through local neighborhoods. The Spring Breakers became disenchanted with Ormond Beach and fled to the panhandle. The baby furniture store went under.

• • •

Allie and I spent many passages of our childhood looking out of windows, watching for people arriving or departing. We were transported, deported, and handed between our parents like crates of Honeycrisp apples.

Thursday was Dad's day with us and, each week, we anchored ourselves to the sidewalk at parent pickup, huddled beneath a metal overhang in the mercy of shade. In the moments before he collected us, the integration of two emotions mishmashed in my gut: excitement and fear. Each emotion was indistinguishable separately. Excitement meant fear. Fear equaled excitement.

The sun sparkled on the hood of his gold Lincoln Town Car rolling through the lot. Allie and I shouted "Shotgun!" and muscled over one another through traffic. He slid our backpacks from our puny frames, tossed them into the trunk, slapped it shut, and folded us into hugs.

My dad was intent on being his own boss. For work, he traveled around the country selling costume jewelry at trade shows. When he flew into town each week for our visits, we passed the afternoons at one of two places: his rental office or the beach.

If we went to the rental office, it meant hours of stagnation. Though I liked when my Aunt Teresa was there helping sort merchandise from stacked, plastic tubs. She was nice and assigned me and Allie small jobs to keep us busy. Some days Allie and I occupied ourselves by choreographing dances to Mexican songs emanating from an FM radio that sat on the windowsill. We poured over the paper sleeves from inside CDs we found lying somewhere around the office in a heap.

Every so often, I was captivated by a necklace or a ring. Once or twice my dad let me keep something for myself, but it never came for free. Sorting and sorting, I didn't fully understand this discretion, but working hard was important to him and he impressed upon me the exchange of labor for profit.

Dad's residences while visiting us were various. Most often, he rented hotel rooms, but usually from the same establishment: a salt caked, white cement building that loomed over the ocean called Pirate's Cove. Here, the afternoon sun slotted through oceanfront condos, striping the beach. Much like costume jewelry, we too were coated in gold. The ebbing daylight glazed the boniness of our curled spines as we stooped to our knees, architecting sandcastles beside the water. Dad skilled us and we marveled as he drizzled, sculpted, and engineered pinnacles, towers, and spires, with mud dripping from his tan, weather-beaten hands. If we skipped afternoons at the office and went straight to the beach, we swam, rode boogie boards, and traced our silhouettes in the sand while holding hands in campy arrangements.

Whenever he rented one-bedroom apartments for longer periods of time, they were always vacant, except for the bedroom that housed a single bed and a TV on a stand. Eventually, he purchased two plushy, child-sized armchairs from the local Walmart that unfolded into beds. At night, Allie and I slept on these in the living room under a sheet. For dinner, we went to chain restaurants for pizza, or we cooked spaghetti with sauce from a jar at the apartment—simple things. After dinner, when night collapsed on us, my dad turned into something else.

• • •

My father's uncontrollable monologues that came at night followed the programming of a classical music composition, divided into three parts: the Exposition, Development, and Recapitulation.

I noted: *A beer in hand. TV volume lowering.* During the Exposition, I was animalistically intuitive at interpreting sequential behavioral clues. These were lights flickering in an auditorium. The orchestral string section readied their bows. On cue, the theme of his harangue was presented. *Ah, a timeless classic: the divorce from our mother.* He called us over to wherever he was seated. His tone wavered between placid and introductory, sometimes amused.

"You know," he'd start, "when I married your mother, I thought we were indestructible. But she wasn't the woman I thought she was."

Over the course of twenty minutes, hitching on particular plot points of their relationship, the lecture escalated into the Development phase. The beastly gnashing of this eventuality was scary and dramatic. The choir crescendoed, brass horns seared the air, spittle flew. When the speech became violent and cutting, threatening and perverse, spewing claims to kill our mom, I shrieked defensive rebuttals at him to "stop!" in a teeny tiny voice. To this, he tossed his head back and laughed; I was a miniature David slinging pitiful pebbles at a raging Goliath. He leaned in closer, reddened, and enunciated the claims.

Allie and I hid from him wherever we could. We shrunk smaller and smaller into microscopic fragments of pulp dust. We reduced our dimensions enough to slide into the narrow space between the bed pushed up against the wall. Or used our own bodies for shelter like petals wilting over one another in a corner—tender mammals.

The eye of his own storm, he seethed from room to room, the fleshiness of his cheeks a severe shade of rose. Our only agency was time. Like weathering a Florida hurricane, we waited him out. His fury, he said, was a testament to the legitimacy and specialness of his *love* and *heartbreak*. We noted this: *excitement:fear:love:pain*.

When he slowed to the final stage, the Recapitulation, he sat on the bed and called to us. We approached trepidatiously. He grabbed the sleeves of our oversized pajama T-shirts and pulled us onto his lap. I couldn't look him in the face. He pressed my head into his chest, which smelled of salt and sweat—a scent I will never forget. "You know I love you," he murmured, kissing the tops of our heads, bringing the composition to a controlled close. Afterward, week to week, we brushed our teeth, climbed under our sheets, and went to sleep.

In the morning, he burst into the living room, cupped a fist to his mouth, and made trumpet sounds as if we were at summer camp. He laughed after he did this and we smiled too, rubbing the sleep from our eyes. Overnight, Allie and I had magically reinflated to our regular, human dimensions. We drifted around the morning apartment in our huge T-shirts like tired ghosts in wretched ball gowns, pouring cereal into bowls from small, one-person portioned boxes. When it was time to do my hair, Dad palmed it into a ponytail and raked its thickness with a men's boar-hair brush. He secured it into a stinging knot with a fat rubber band.

On the silent drive to daycare, a hangover from the previous night's devastation clung to us. The psychological impacts of flagrant badmouthing between parents, directed through children, are severe. Repetitively, these impacts printed on me. I couldn't feel my brain changing in real time, though it was. Children view themselves as made up of equal parts of both parents—half and half—and when one parent puts down the other, they are incidentally putting down their child too.[4] Assumptions of my own despicability unconsciously braided through me.

Our relationships with our parents are primordial ones that set the tone for all subsequent relationships in life.[5] My path was cast.

Unwittingly, I gazed through the broad windshield, shivered from the air conditioning in my magenta windbreaker, and drifted to a different place in my mind. I imagined how the car, with its long, broad hood, resembled the jaws of a crocodile of which we were trapped inside, viewing the world from behind its eyes.

A smiling teacher greeted us at daycare in a front room and my dad signed us in. Allie and I entered, turned a corner, and climbed onto a bench, taking our post at the window facing the main road. Our Friday morning ritual, side by side, we watched Dad's Town Car recede from view. I felt tremendously sad watching my dad leave: this complicated person who built extravagant sand castles with me. *Where is he going?* I asked myself. While Thursdays and Fridays he was with us, the other days of the week were mysterious unknowns.

---

4 "Why Badmouthing the Other Parent Hurts Your Child," Beyond Words, accessed January 7, 2021.

5 Eckhart Tolle, *A New Earth: Awakening to Your Life's Purpose* (New York: Viking Press, 2005) 100.

I didn't know it at the time, but my mom had consulted a lawyer on what she could do about the visitation rights my father was legally righted to. The lawyer told her if her children were not showing obvious signs of distress, like acting out in school or failing grades, there was nothing she could do.

The trouble is that children faced with family dysfunction tend to fall into five, potentially overlapping, archetypes, four of which—hero, clown, lost child, and rescuer—outwardly reflect high achievement, humor, quietude, and perfectionism.[6]

At the end of the day Mom retrieved us. Allie and I shuffled into her six-seater van that whisked us to our three-bedroom house pushed back in the woody neighborhood. My dad asserts he built our house brick by brick through back-breaking labor. Mom says they hired a contractor, but Dad laid the kitchen tiles.

We dropped our backpacks on the kitchen table.

"Well," Mom said, pulling a bag of grapes from the refrigerator, "how was it?"

I looked up at her. "It was okay." I shrugged. "We went to the beach."

She set the grapes on the counter and folded her arms over her chest. "Did he say anything nasty about me?"

I searched my feet. "He was really angry last night. Yelling again."

"What did he say?" she pressed.

A tight thing pulled in my stomach, like a drawstring compressing the opening of a fabric sack. Allie escaped into her bedroom faster than me, and I hated being the

---

6 Alexandra Massey, "What Are the Dysfunctional Family Archetypal Rules and Roles?" AlexandraMassey.co.uk (blog), updated June 10, 2020.

correspondent for these briefings, which pinned me, again, at the center of my parents' contention.

I tilted my head back and cringed into the skylight, trying to remember the highlights. "Uh... He said something like you were two champion horses in a race. But that um... you used to be on a team. And now you're not? Or like his horse fell and broke its leg? I don't know."

"What!" she interrupted incredulously. She laughed and tossed some grapes into her mouth.

"Well," I stressed, "he told us he's going to *bury* you six feet *underground.*" My eyes watered.

She drew backward and clucked her tongue, appalled. "He's an asshole," she stated conclusively, nodding and chewing another grape. Then she kneeled down on the tile floor, eye level with me. "You know what I always say? Just let it go through one ear and out the other."

• • •

My dad was indelicate with us. Excitement is fear, love is pain.

In 1994, my mom, Allie, and I ran into my dad in the lobby of a beachside hotel. The hotel hosted a timeshare my parents purchased while they were married. We frequented the resort so often the chef of the poolside restaurant hung a photograph of me and Allie in the dining room. One day, while checking in, my dad walked right past us. It was the first time I'd ever encountered my father as a stranger—a separate entity from me—in public. Spotting us, he froze. The receptionist handed the day-access key over the counter to my mother and she, seeing him, pulled Allie and me by our wrists toward the electric doors that swung open to the pool deck. I felt stunned seeing my father just a few yards away and not being able to run to him. I was shaken by his uncharacteristic calm.

A few hours later, we packed up our things, checked out with the receptionist, and climbed into the van. The engine sputtered when Mom turned the key. She tried a few more times. Nothing. She called AAA and we waited for them in the sun for two hours. It was too brutally hot to sit inside the van, so we stood beside it on the black asphalt that burned our feet through plastic flip flops. When the technician arrived, he was disturbed to report someone had filled our entire gas tank with sand.

My dad challenged gender norms with his Christmas gifts back in 1995, purchasing unlikely gifts for small girls, such as hockey sets and baseball bats. *At least we'll be well rounded,* I supposed. *At least we'll be* tough. One Christmas, he surprised us with a gun. He drove us across his apartment complex to a vacant lot and set up some cans a few yards away on a fence post. I was six and too scared to shoot it. Allie went first. He arranged the gun on her shoulder and helped her index finger draw the trigger back. The BB bullet ripped through the barrel, ricocheted off a fence beam, and struck Allie in the collar bone. He picked her up and squeezed her into a hug. She buried her face in the bulk of his jean jacket, but it didn't do much to muffle her screaming.

In the summer of 1997, Dad took us on a getaway to the Florida Keys. I'd never been to Key West before and was mesmerized by the saturation of its hues against the clearness of the water. In the morning, he rented a small catamaran; we packed a cooler with snacks and set out to sea. By 4:00 p.m., we were lost and the catamaran was lodged on a coral reef. Shoulders reddened, Allie and I tucked our knees to our chests and waited patiently.

"Hand me my shoes," said my dad. I did and he yanked them onto his bare, callused feet. Before he clambered over the side of the boat into the ocean, he looked at us and said "this reef is gonna cut the shit out of me." He plunged into the water, tugging and rocking the boat loose. The waves dusted with crimson as Staghorn coral stabbed through his sneakers.

That same evening, on shore, we lounged in peace on a dock behind our hotel. I stood up and scuffed my feet over the dock planks until reaching the very edge of it. I curled my toes over the side. I bowed my head and examined the rippling echo of my likeness superimposed on the water's surface. Tilting slightly forward, I felt butterflies.

"Go ahead!" my dad shouted playfully from somewhere behind. "Jump!"

I was afraid of heights. I could barely climb the stairs at waterparks, frightened the paper thinness of me would slip through the gaps in the steps, and I'd plummet to my death. "I'm scared!" I yelled. I swiveled around to face him, but only made it ninety degrees when his hands forced into me.

As I fell from the dock, I instinctively completed the rotation, reaching my arms out to grab hold of something behind me. The corner of a metal sign bolted to the wooden pile caught my twisted ribcage and slashed into my torso. Like his ankles on the reef, a colossus of rouge blossomed into the water's clarity. My father sprinted down the boat ramp, extracted my body, and wrapped it in a starched, white hotel towel that soaked with blood. He cradled me into his chest, dashed through the hotel lobby, up the stairs, opened the door to our room, and placed me in the bathtub.

• • •

For some reason, it'd never occurred to me to ask how the separation between my parents transpired. So, when I was twenty-eight years old, I asked my mom. *What did the finer details—moving out of the house and dividing children—look like?*

She told me that on a weekend afternoon they got into a fight. As was his nature, when the argument cooled my dad became loving and affectionate. Before he could ask my mother for intimacy, she said "I need to go out for some groceries." She buckled Allie and me into our car seats in the back of the van. She drove to an underground women's shelter and never came back.

2

SHAPES

My dad was six feet tall. His hair was light brown and curly, and his nose had the slightest crook. His cheeks were high and positioned beneath almond eyes. While charming, something broiled under the surface and, like synapses, it released in gesticulations.

My mom was five feet and four inches tall. She too had small eyes and curly hair, but her hair was shiny and black. Her nose was straight, but pronounced at the tip, and her smile was warm. She was a little introverted, but friendly.

Both of my parents had New York accents.

When my parents started dating other people, I didn't think much about the impact of this landmark turning point. I did, however, observe the human samples they presented to us as potential suitors with a critical eye, unintentionally testing their stress thresholds. My body was a bomb, or a pop quiz, ready to detonate or audition their aptitudes as guardians in a moment's notice.

One woman my father introduced us to had two sons who were a year or two older than Allie and me. My dad seemed to like this woman because we spent more time at her house than with any of his other girlfriends. Her name was Carly, and I thought her son closest to my age was cute. Both sons were fascinated by Allie.

When my body was eight years old, it was four and a half feet tall and weighed forty-five pounds. It was a very bony and nimble body. The whole thing was very geometric looking—even my face. Like Dad, I had small, half-moon shaped eyes, high cheekbones, and a slight crook in my nose. Even my hair was geometric. When its mass wasn't bundled into a bun, it bulked out to my shoulders in a frizzy isosceles triangle and its porous texture absorbed the light—an optical phenomenon.

Years later, in college, I was so self-conscious of my nose crook I exhaustively researched rhinoplasty on the internet. In my search, I discovered the scientific name for a nose crook is called a "dorsal hump." "Dorsal" is also the word used to describe the curved fin on the back of a dolphin, allowing the animal to maintain stability as it glides through water. For weeks, I was unable to consider my nose as anything other than a sail attached to my face. I've never consciously implemented it for its Darwinian strengths, like using it to glide quickly through crowded airports or courtyards.

At nine years old, my sister's body was not quite as skinny as mine, but not much thicker either. She was slightly taller than me and had long, shiny, straight brown hair that reflected the light, and hung perfectly around her conventionally beautiful face. She had bright, average sized eyes; a sharp, straight nose; and perfectly set teeth.

While Allie had an easiness, flirtatiousness, and feminine charm, my disposition around the opposite sex was like a shrunken version of the character Alvy Singer from the movie *Annie Hall.* Quietly neurotic, I was shy, sensitive, both terrified of and desperate for attention. Below the waist,

I donned the thickest, baggiest, most impenetrable blue jeans imaginable. Jeans so heavy they could trap a speeding bullet. I covered myself on top with oversized cotton t-shirts. Overconfident phrases were stitched into the fronts, like "All Star" and "Hottie." The look was completed by a pair of hiking boots. I offered no small talk or sweet talk to conversations, but a whole lotta talk on the Brachiosaurus Rex.

One boiling afternoon, Allie, the brothers, and I played tag in Carly's front yard while she and Dad relaxed inside the house. We squared each other and my sister pointed at me and pronounced "You're it!" I visibly deflated. I hated being "it." I was the youngest, the smallest, and therefore the slowest. Chasing them to no fruitful end was daunting, and it embarrassed me in front of the younger brother.

I wiped sweat from my forehead and begrudgingly accepted my appointment. I lurched into action and they bolted in a dispersion around the corner of the house. After a full loop around the front and backyard I stopped to catch my breath beside a wooden post lodged in the ground. Someone jogged up on me from behind, and I turned. It was Allie. Seeing me resting, her expression formed into one of annoyance, then distorted into disturbance. I followed her gaze to my shoes. Beyond my heaving chest a pandemonium of red dots streamed over my sneakers, my socks, and up my shins. Like two torches, my legs began to burn.

"You're in an ant pile!" Allie screeched.

Emitting an ear-splitting scream, the front door of the house burst open. Dad bounded toward me, abducted me from the pile, carried me into Carly's bathroom, and soaked my clothing through with cold water exploding from the shower head. We went home shortly thereafter. I didn't see Carly or her sons much after that.

• • •

When school was out, Allie and I spent a lot of time with our grandparents. My grandpa was an animated, performative Italian man who liked to make us laugh and my grandmother was a quiet, petite Italian woman who spent a lot of time in the kitchen. Afternoons ticked by at their house watching movies, swimming in their pool, or playing solitaire on their desktop computer. Occasionally, my grandma arranged us a snack: sliced apples dusted with cinnamon or an entire head of cold, raw cabbage. I didn't exactly know how to eat the cabbage, as biting into a spherical vegetable the size of my cranium felt counterintuitive. If I asked, she would slice it into halves—one for me and one for Allie—and even shook some pepper on it. *Buon appetito!*

I delighted in watching my grandfather putter around in the warmth of his garage. The garage door was always open and the smell of damp soil and river water rushed in from the outside. Tacked on the walls all around us, tools were slung or dangled from straps. Wooden corn cob pipes and dirty rags scattered his work station. I liked the smell of tobacco and oil on him. In all the summers I observed his tinkering, I can't recall anything specific he repaired; however, he always maintained a generic air of industriousness.

He kept a gigantic plastic tub on a metal shelf filled with chalk for us, which Allie and I scraped down to stubs, leaving the contours of our imaginations all along the driveway. He sat on a stool, smoked a cigar, and chortled as we dipped plastic bubble wands into an inverted frisbee filled with dish soap. We slashed our arms across the air, filling the wands with tremendous bubbles that we burst by biting straight through their liquid walls or by clapping our arms down shut on them like a voracious maw.

My grandfather wore a lot of polo shirts. We dipped into his closet once and counted over three hundred. When we played monopoly at the dining room table, which lasted for hours, our reward at the end of the game was to destroy one of the shirts. When the game finished, Allie and I climbed to a standing position on our chairs. We locked eyes across the dining room table. It was *time.* We jumped up and down and cried "Rip the shirt! Rip the shirt! Please please please *pleasepleasepleaseplease* can we rip a shirt?"

Grandpa, amused, modestly excused himself to the bedroom. He returned a minute later wearing a different shirt, one *thoughtfully* selected and regarded as expendable—a corporeal sacrifice. He resumed position in his chair. Then he gave the signal. "Go!" We leapt from our chairs, latched onto the shirt sleeves with measly fists, and pulled the seams until the shirt began to tear.

The roar of popping threads was euphoric. My grandfather thrashed his arms slowly, imitating King Kong. "Roooooarrrrr!" he roared, curling his hands like talons. Allie and I squealed with glee, high on utter destruction. We roved around the shirt like wolves, refusing to cease until the shirt was torn ragged, hanging from his torso like a rag. The robustness of his chest hair and gold necklaces exposed. He howled laughing at the absurdity, and, when we were satisfied with the carnage, he removed the shirt and threw it in the kitchen trash.

The quietness of their house accentuated our aliveness. From a little wooden radio on a shelf in the den, he played music for us from the 1960's. We vaulted ourselves onto the leather couch and leapt crisscross from one cushion to the other, then to the floor, and back again as The Angels' "My boyfriend's Back" crooned through the radio speakers. I had no idea what it was like to have a boyfriend, but I banged my head and pictured myself on the back of a motorcycle with someone who looked like John Travolta.

Some afternoons, I tiptoed through the master bedroom and into the bathroom unnoticed. I slid the bathroom door shut behind me and stared into the mirror filling the grooves in the bathmat from where my grandmother usually stood—a genetic extension of her, an echo, a perennial. I kept the overhead lights off, and filtered sunlight from the skylight above softened the room. Hoisting myself onto the cold, marble countertop, I picked up her silver lipstick tubes one by one, pulling the metal tops off and clicking them back on. I disassembled her eye shadow palettes, examining the blue powder frosting on the foam applicator tips.

The vanity was recessed into the wall. When I pressed my back against one end of the mirror and looked across the vanity toward the other end, the mirror facing me reflected back my image but also the mirror behind me, which positioned me in a vortex. I shifted silently in its kaleidoscopic prisms, wondering which portals I was on the precipice of tumbling into. My grandparent's house was another dimension—a place impartial to the outside world, a place unquestionably safe. Allie and I expanded into the freedom of our weirdness and wildness within the security of its container. Outside of the container was chaos.

Though getting by financially as a single-parent household, time as a resource with our mom was scant. Efficiency was of value. For example, every Sunday morning my mom dropped Allie and I off at our hour-long catechism classes after church. Then she raced home in her car to mow the lawn for thirty minutes. When finished, she raced back to the church to collect us after class. My grandparents' free childcare services helped to offset our living expenses, and their familiarity kept everyone feeling secure, which was a privilege.

At the time, there were sixteen million single-mother households in America—a number steadily rising since 1970.[7] I recently asked my mom if she felt overburdened as a single parent and she said "I was tired, but I was lucky. I wouldn't have made it without my parents." She nudged the glasses at the bridge of her nose with her finger. "There was one woman who I worked with at the post office, also recently divorced, who *didn't* have anyone to watch her children. And she couldn't afford childcare. During our shifts together, she rolled down the windows to her car in the employee parking lot and that's where her children waited for her." She shrugged. "What else could she do?"

Mom picked us up after work and took us home. She fed and prepared us for bed. Sometimes she laid alongside me reading stories from picture books. I liked when she brought bright colored plastic cups of water to leave for me on the bedside. She put her face close to mine and whispered God's plan. Not the cliché plan the church exploited to everyone, but the *real* plan of what transpired in baby factories in the sky. "When babies are ready to come down to earth," she whispered "they're put on an assembly line. Everybody gets a sprinkle of niceness, sweetness, smartness, and cuteness."

"But *then*..." her whisper intensified, "there must have been a hiccup in the factory. And you got a little extra of *everything*." She kissed my forehead, rose from the bed, and turned out the light. I loved burning the craziness out of

---

7 Statista, "Number of Children Living with a Single Mother or a Single Father in the US from 1970 to 2019," last modified November 2019.

my contents at my grandparent's house, but cherished the intimacy with my mother at night.

• • •

Mom was also dating, but it took a while before we met the man who became our stepfather. He was tall, blonde, and mild mannered. Quiet, but kind.

When things were getting serious, my mother brought Allie and I to his house to introduce us. We stood in the foyer and shyly milled about. Allie asked where the bathroom was and disappeared into a bedroom, abandoning me. She stuck her head through the doorframe and gave me a look imploring me to follow her. She led me through the bedroom into a private bathroom.

She closed the door behind us and turned to face a little table next to the toilet paper dispenser. "Look at *that*," she said and pointed. I looked. "It's a cactus."

I moved toward it.

"Don't touch it!"

I reached out my hand.

"Don't!" she asserted.

I picked the little cactus up by the ceramic base and ran two fingers from my other hand over the smooth, waxy cactus skin, in between the translucent spines.

She moved in closer and ran a finger over it too. "Ow!" She flinched, then raised her fingers to eye level.

I inspected the domes of my fingertips too. Billions of microscopic cactus spines stippled the skin. We panicked. I set the cactus down on the table and we took turns pinching spines from one another's fingers to no avail. She rubbed her hands against her backside anxiously, hoping the friction against her fabric leggings would pull the spines loose from the skin. I did the same. Soon we had cactus spines in our fingers, in our palms, and in our butts.

"Are you guys okay?" I heard my mom call from the other side of the door.

Allie and I exchanged distressed glances. Mom pushed the door open. She and my future stepfather stood in the frame, looking like a contemporary *American Gothic*. We shot our prickly palms overhead in surrender. My future stepdad produced some tweezers from a cabinet and he and Mom spent the rest of the afternoon picking spines from our buttocks.

Like an amoeba, relatives revolved solidly around Allie and me at the center, but the family was changing shape around the edges. My parents' relationship was fractured in half, but those halves were propagating.

3

DESIRE

I watched the September 11 terrorist attacks on the World Trade Center in 2001 live on a television set that was rolled to the front of my sixth-grade algebra class. The footage was chilling and unreal. My teacher was solemn for the full class hour, and when he turned the television off, we sat in silence. The principal's aid knocked on the door of our portable to collect the students whose parents called to pick them up early. The rest of us, disturbed but confused, passed notes, stared at our desks, and waited patiently for instructions from the principal.

America's invasion of Afghanistan to dismantle the Taliban regime lasted only two months, but the ongoing war to defeat a Taliban insurgency and rebuild core institutions of the Afghan state lasted until 2008. Insurgent attacks and civilian casualties remained stubbornly high until 2012. When the US and NATO ended their combat mission in 2014, I had already graduated from college. As the longest war in American history, its longevity made it, in some ways, a desensitized backdrop to millennial, American life.[8]

---

8 G. Witte, "Afghanistan War," Encyclopedia Britannica, October 31, 2020.

My parents and I didn't speak about the attacks much when they happened. I pieced together my basic understanding of it through context clues. Repercussions beyond the initial devastation—national xenophobia, post-traumatic stress, late onset illnesses from toxic dust and residue—were lost on me. One evening, my mom left me in the car to collect Allie from her evening jazz class. She left the radio on. I listened closely to the broadcaster report details of bombings over the Middle East, killing civilians. I smoothed the word *civilians* over in my mind, processing its meaning. Sensitized in the dark, I looked across the parking lot and imagined what it might be like to live in a place where my mom and sister were at risk of obliteration by walking from the dance studio to the car.

When they swung open the car doors, the overhead light flicked on. "Why are you crying?" asked my mom.

"I don't know," I said.

In November of 2001, President Bush signed the Aviation and Transportation Security Act (TSA).[9] My mom applied for a job as a TSA agent to help screen passengers and their bags before boarding airplanes. She accepted the pay cut and quit her job at the post office. I was delighted by the stories she came home with of what she found in people's luggage. Like severed alligator heads wrapped in trash bags, whole blocks of cheese, or pornographic materials. Still, when she tried to explain that her job was searching for bombs, this was too big a concept for me to grasp, and it became desensitized too.

I viewed the event of September 11 through a childish veil of separation. I viewed the attacks as though they were

---

9 "Timeline: Aviation and Transportation Security Act," Homeland Security Digital Library, accessed January 9, 2021.

unrelated to me by way of physical distance and complexity, even though they reverberated into our living room, cloaked my mother in uniform, paid our electric bill, and put food on our table. I wasn't aware of my national or global identities yet, and my responsibilities based on those identities, that are assigned to all of us just by being born.

• • •

In 2002, two boys moved into my neighborhood just around the corner. Their names were Chris and Sean. They were twins.

Chris and Sean were tall, white as specters, skeletal, pimply, and brunette. They were unenthusiastic, exhibiting nearly insentient apathy, which made them totally invulnerable. If a show of amusement occurred, their bared teeth sparkled behind a gridlock of metal braces. Their laughter was expressed in low, restricted chortling. They were received by their peers as exotic and sought-after bachelors.

For convenience, the bus driver declared my driveway the neighborhood bus stop, where all the kids should gather in the morning. Bearing the weight of such responsibility caused me anxiety. I didn't know a thing about hospitality! Though it wouldn't have made a difference if I did. The twins' coolness was so steely, if I had exploded from my house on roller blades, rolled down the driveway wielding a tray of bourbon shots on fire, and shot bottle rockets from between my teeth, they wouldn't have batted an eye.

Each morning they showed up dull-eyed, backpacks dangling like pendants over one shoulder because they couldn't be bothered to use both straps. Allie and I walked outside to wait with them. I dropped my own backpack the size of a hard-top sedan on the wet cement, the jostling of my pens and spiral notebooks interrupting the loaded silence. A neighbor girl joined us, and she and Allie paired off. They swiveled roller ball glitter sticks over their arms and cleavage while Chris and Sean observed. I rolled my eyes. It wasn't enough witnessing Allie repeatedly rewarded for her beauty with affection and popularity, now she was literally shimmering. I despised what I deemed this as, which was superficial approval seeking. Glaring at them I vowed *I will never stoop so low as to pursue attention with such cheap and obvious means.*

I slid a dollar bill for my lunch money from my pocket and flattened it with my fingers. Fiddling with it absentmindedly, I listened for the bus.

"Hey," Sean said. "Can I see that?"

I looked up. "Why?"

"Because," he said. "I'll show you something cool. I know how to fold it so it looks like the Twin Towers."

I mirrored his impassiveness, turning the dollar over in my hands.

"Can I see it?" he insisted. I handed it to him.

Sean flexed the dollar bill into origami-like arrangements with his bony fingers. Chris watched at his shoulder. After two minutes he held it up at eye level.

"See," Sean said coolly, pointing to a crease. "You kinda lose a little bit of it here, but doesn't it look like them? Here's one tower and there's the other."

I studied the dollar. Then I heard my mouth say, "Yea, now you just need to set it on fire."

The twins identically recoiled and gawked in my direction. Then I heard it. Their chortling. They ogled me admirably. My unexpected edginess had earned their praises, an extraordinary feat. In middle school sarcasm was king.

I'd imagined what the sheer bliss of their approval might feel like, but I felt no such thing as bliss. I felt sickened. My stomach lurched at the distastefulness of what I blurted out. I was surprised and ashamed by my own capacity for callousness. *How did I arrive so quickly to such a vile critique? Am I evil? Am I wrought with unseeable pockets of insensitive remarks?*

I was a sellout, pliable to the seduction of admiration. Except I wasn't inclined toward passive tools like glitter sticks, but the potent tool of language. I didn't speak again until the bus came.

• • •

I sat beside my best friend Maggie toward the middle of the bus. She lived in the neighborhood across from mine in a newly built house tripling the size of my own. Maggie was my height, race, and weight, but blonde and grumpy. The twins headed to the back of the bus with my sister and her older friends, where it reeked of cheap body lotions with too sweet titles of food combinations that I would never apply to my body in real life, like Banana Buttercream, Cool Mulberry Melon, Pound Cake, Cashmere Coconut, and Candied yams.

At school, Maggie, the twins, and I filtered into Homeroom. As the twins had secured girlfriends quickly, the four of them sat together as a pod during morning announcements. The girlfriends looked nothing like me or Maggie. They were petite and we were tall. They had shiny, straight hair, we had frizzy, curly hair. They had big eyes, we had small eyes. They were topped off with button noses and coquettish grace, and we had crooked noses and spent our weekends digging up deer skulls in the backwoods with our bare hands.

Most girls admitted to having crushes on Chris and Sean and, like Jane Goodall, I studied how they interacted with their female counterparts. Maggie said she didn't have a crush on them, but I sensed that she did and that she felt an abyssal rejection by the twins' indifference to her, which was hurtful and confusing.

Desire takes many shapes. While I made sense of my own unrequited love, and the rejection of it, by placing the brothers on a pedestal, Maggie distanced herself from her feelings through loathing by rejecting what rejected her.

"They're not even pretty," she muttered about the girlfriends, scratching at her binder on the ride home from school with a blue pen. Our knees pressed into the back of the warm, brown, leather bus seat. We slouched over our notebooks resting open on our thighs. "They're actually kind of ugly. Kerry has those long eyelashes. She looks like a barn animal. Have you noticed?"

Her question was rhetorical. Even though I was envious of the girlfriends, I actually kind of liked them. Or I didn't mind them, at least. I found them friendly and approachable.

"And Melissa," she continued, "I can barely even see what she looks like with all those disgusting freckles."

She cackled and slapped her hand on her binder, eyes crinkling at the corners. I smiled weakly. I only saw Maggie get excited when she was up to something devious or ridiculing someone. I was curious, which made me devious, but I didn't naturally take to ridiculing others. I believed I was immune.

I got off the bus at Maggie's house that Friday afternoon. Maggie's mother was a hairdresser and was home most of the time. She was like helium: buoyant, blonde, and dim-witted. She had a nice laugh and tipped her head fondly when she spoke to me. As nice and hospitable as her mom was, and even though she gave Maggie anything she asked for, Maggie hated her.

Maggie's dad was the opposite of her mom. He was like chromium: loaded and dense. A stern man with a handlebar mustache. He was a chemical engineer and I only saw him in the evenings after work. When he barked at Maggie to turn off light switches or take her laundry out of the dryer, he jabbed the air threateningly with his middle finger extended. Maggie hated him too.

Maggie's dad bought her mom a Rolls-Royce that we weren't allowed to touch, as not to leave spots on the wax job. Whenever we rode in it, I was unsure of how to open the doors without touching the handles. After dinner, her mom drove us to a nearby video store to rent a DVD. We chose a campy horror film called *Lake Placid*, which starred a thirty-foot-long saltwater crocodile that terrorized a dysfunctional group of twenty-somethings attempting to capture and kill it.

When Maggie's parents went to sleep, we put the movie on in the spare bedroom. Snuggled under crocheted blankets, we howled at busty women's heads flying off, severed by the crocodile, and forced handfuls of popcorn down our throats. "I wish that was Kerry," Maggie jeered, molars gnashing over kernels. "Wait." She stiffened. The blue light streamed over her expression. She turned to face me. "Let's make voodoo dolls. Do you want to?"

My deviousness teased to the surface. "Yes," I hissed.

She tossed off the blanket and disappeared from the room. She tiptoed back in carrying two bars of soap and a spoon and dropped them on the carpet in between us. "I'll make Kerry and you make Melissa," she whispered. We tore open the soap boxes and pulled out the waxy white ovals from inside. Our silhouettes hunched in front of the television, chipping away at the soaps, carving eyes, noses, and mouths, bobbling lightly and snickering.

By Monday morning the emotional charge behind the voodoo doll making was gone. It was just a funny memory. The soap turned out to be harder to manipulate than we anticipated. Before we went to sleep, we'd broken the soap bars into chunks that we threw into the toilet, flushing the evidence. I didn't think about it as I set my backpack down at my desk and walked across the room toward the pencil sharpener. So did Kerry. We smiled at each other/

"I was in your neighborhood this weekend," she said, giving me a funny look. "Melissa and I hung out with Chris and Sean."

"Oh!" I rotated the lever that fed my pencil into the steampunk looking at the machine gnawing at it like a wood chipper. "Was it fun?" I asked politely.

"Yeah! Their house is really nice." She took a step closer and whispered. "Hey. Can I tell you something?"

I stopped grinding and faced her.

"We played a game this weekend where everyone said who they would go out with if they weren't going out with each other." She pressed her flawless forehead almost against my own. "Chris said he would go out with Dani." She glared at Dani across the room as if Dani had anything to do with it. "But Sean," she beamed "said he would go out with *you*." She raised her eyebrows and skirted past me, inserting her pencil into the wood-chipper.

I couldn't focus for the rest of the day. *Me*, I mooned. I couldn't believe it. No one I liked had ever liked me back before, only the boys I didn't desire. This was a fresh feeling, to be liked, to be *noticed*. My insides were gooey. Though, how Kerry had disclosed the information made it feel very private, very special, very secret. I didn't want to be a homewrecker, so I kept it to myself. I told no one.

I stared out the window on the bus ride home, asking myself *How will this transform me?* My love was in fact not unrequited. Acknowledgment felt *good.* I was used to receding into the background unnoticed, behind Allie's beauty, behind the bounty of Maggie's family money.

Though, every thought of Sean was trailed by a thought of Melissa. Something wasn't clicking, like misdirected fuses. Sean liked her, but also *me.* How could I ever actualize my love for *him* if he was with *her*? Despite the voodoo dolls, I wished her no real harm. But something had to give.

When I got home, I went to my room and closed the door. I removed my sneakers, socks, jeans, and laid on the carpet in my underwear and T-shirt. I picked a gel pen up off the floor and twirled it between my fingers. I repeated his name in my mind like a melody, *Sean... Sean... Sean...*

What if being second best to Melissa isn't so bad? I thought. *It's almost* more *romantic this way. He and I have a secret. A forbidden desire.* I'd seen this type of romantic tension in movies before, like in *Grease*—between Sandy and Danny—or in *Clueless*—between Cher and Josh. These templates demonstrated that the protagonists always got what they wanted. They set themselves apart from the competition by holding back and waiting to be recognized.

I uncapped the pen and carefully drew each letter of Sean's name S-E-A-N in glittering, silver gel on the inside of my bicep, where no one would be able to see it. Then I penned it on my other bicep. Then I wrote it on the inside of my thigh. Then on the bottom of my foot. Then between my fingers, and on my belly, and my chest, until my whole body was owned by him. I was covered in silver foil emblems of my dearest beloved, like a Louis Vuitton bag. The laurels of this mythologizing were intoxicating!

Oh, the erotic fairytale, fidelities that could come from desire behind the scenes!

I don't need our love, or myself, on display, I thought, rolling around in my filthy zeal. *No no no, this is* good, *this is* better. *A behind the scenes tryst! There is passion and integrity in being second best.*

4

SUSPENSE

My parents worked out an arrangement where Allie and I lived full-time with Mom during the school year, and one month of the summer with my dad in Illinois with him and my stepmom. When the time came to make the switch, we either flew to him on an airplane, or he picked us up in Florida and drove us back to the Midwest. If we traveled by car we listened to music, stopped at small landmarks of interest, and slept in hotels along the way.

Money was magic around my dad. He enjoyed lecturing me on where to find it and which schemes were most effective in getting it. We never seemed to have enough of it, and yet it flourished around us all the time. Though the idea of working hard was significant to him, his aspirations inclined toward a life of unyielding prosperity, so that he wouldn't work at all. It didn't make sense to me. If he loved chasing money so much, what was he going to do with himself if he wasn't working? Additionally, his obsession with transcending the grind only seemed to cause more grinding.

When we were tight on money, I sensed it by how selective we were at grocery stores. Though it was difficult to tell. When he was in the mood to spend, he was extravagant, treating the family to crustaceous feasts—arriving home with bags of steaming crab legs and lobster tails. We sat on his leather couches, jovial and bantering, TV trays propped open before us, plastic bibs squeezing our necks and catching the bits of crab meat slipping from our buttered fingers.

After several trips by car between Illinois and Florida, he bought an RV. We stuffed the RV's guts with endless tools to cure boredom during long stretches of highway. A TV and VCR were positioned above the helm of the driver's seat and we filled an overhead cubby with VHS tapes. We kept crayons, colored pencils, coloring books, and a card deck in a hollowed bench seat. Allie and I ran into the back, peeking out of windows at passing cars. We held up nonsensical messages scrawled in crayon. We made our teddy bears wave at children in vehicles moving in sync alongside us.

When my father, stepmother, cousin, sister, and I traveled in the RV together, the limited quarters made intimacy and controversy interchangeably accessible. Sometimes we occupied ourselves simply through bickering. At least one person cried a day. I escaped into the fantasy of books.

We visited many places together though the Midwest and East Coast, like Jekyll Island, Georgia and Indiana's Dunes State park. We slept in campsites, Flying J truck-stops or Walmart parking lots. There wasn't enough space for five people to sleep, so I made a bed on the dashboard because I was the smallest.

Whenever we slept at truck stops, loudspeakers blared into the parking lot all night long, announcing time slots for the indoor showers.

Whenever we slept in Walmart parking lots, my stepmom disappeared after dinner and reappeared with plastic bags of matching gifts—mugs, towels, or shower caddies. My cousin and sister received pink and I received purple or blue.

Whenever we slept in campsites, my cousin, sister, and I walked around at night mingling with teenagers and lying about our ages. We ate hot dogs and marshmallows over campfires.

I observed the effects alcohol played on our family dynamic—how things seemed to unravel in its presence, and usually at night. Unease around security presented when the authority went rogue. Spats between my dad and stepmom broke out and, fifty percent of the time, they combusted and the arguing escalated from one pitch to the next. There may have been a time or two when someone threatened suicide with the loaded gun my father kept on him. And then, *just like that*, the next day things were peachy. We were snacking on peanut butter and jelly sandwiches on an idyllic beach, like a living impressionist painting.

Over the years, the repeated pattern of being cornered in spaces with intense storms of fighting, over-stimulation, and breaches of security altered my nervous system. I vacillated between chronic states of hypersensitivity and numbing. These effects were not unique to me. Complexly traumatized youth frequently suffer from body dysregulation, meaning they overrespond or under respond to sensory stimuli.[10] They may be hypersensitive to sounds, smells, touch, or light. Or, conversely, they may suffer from depersonalization and dissociation, in which the mind goes blank, majorly decreasing activation in every area.[11]

I interpreted these abilities as *superpowers*.

With hypersensitive intuition on the verge of clairvoyance, I existed ten steps ahead of everyone around me. Or, when danger

---

10 "Complex Trauma: Effects," The National Child Traumatic Stress Network, accessed January 10, 2021.

11 Bessel Van Der Kolk, *The Body Keeps the Score: Brain, Mind, and Body in the Healing of Trauma* (New York: Penguin Books, 2015), 71.

manifested in rages or yelling, I departed from my body. I cast myself into reveries, distracting myself with minutiae. I zoomed way in on things, bewitching myself with the beauty and simplicity of an ant crawling over a stretch of floral wallpaper.

After attending the beach one morning off the coast of Georgia, we trudged over the dunes to the RV, which was parked in a raised lot overlooking the ocean. A storm was rolling in and beachgoers scattered. We washed the sand off of us in the outdoor showers and changed into dry clothes. The sky deepened to indigo.

My abdomen clenched as the wind picked up. Rain battered the windows and the RV rocked from side to side. We sat quietly from different positions, rapt attention directed through the windshield. Thunderbolts pulsed against a backdrop of cumulonimbus clouds, connected with the ocean, and the storm drew closer to our position on the hill. While I was terrified, my father looked charged against the theatrics of the storm.

"It's beautiful, isn't it?" he said, looking straight ahead. I couldn't deny it was.

• • •

My dad had also purchased the RV as a means for traveling to different jewelry shows and flea markets, and sometimes he took us with him. Mostly, we went to Shipshewana, Indiana—the Midwest's largest flea market and the home to the third largest Amish community in the US.[12]

We usually aimed to get there on Friday evenings so we could set up the tent the following morning, as Saturday was the busiest and most profitable day of the week.

---

12 "Visit Shipshewana Indiana," Shipshewana Indiana, accessed January 16, 2021.

The sun smoldered on the horizon as our enormous vehicle rolled past endless swaths of corn stalk, finally pulling into the vacant fairgrounds parking lot. No people, only dirt. Night prevailed and my father cooked spaghetti on the petite RV stove. We ate from plastic dishes and cutlery, and a VHS tape of the Christmas movie *The Family Man* reeled in the VCR for the hundredth time. Our eyes washed in blue light, fixed on the tiny TV screen centered over the dashboard. My sister lounged on the sidelong bench cushion and I perched just outside the door on the hydraulic staircase.

"Did I ever tell you," Dad voiced over the television with his mouth full, "about the time I was in this thing in Arkansas during a tornado?"

We turned and looked at him, still slurping noodles through our puckered lips. We shook our heads no, even though he definitely had.

"The sound," he bugged his eyes, "is *unforgettable*."

Allie scraped her fork against the plastic edge of the bowl and stabbed at the gooey meal with its prongs.

"It was pitch black and I was parked on the side of the road on my way to a convention center in Texas. I was boiling water for spaghetti, just like we are now. And then I heard a train in the distance. But loud. You know what a train sounds like?"

We slurped.

"It's *loud*," he enunciated. "And the whole RV was shaking—like this," he mimicked frenetic motions with his arms raised. "It wasn't a train; it was a tornado! I had to hold onto the pot of boiling water so the damn thing didn't fall off the stove and burn me. I was scared shitless!" He looked forward toward the windshield, let out a dry laugh, and then looked at me. He narrowed his eyes and nodded.

We didn't finish *The Family Man* that night. We cleaned up and folded the dining table down into a converted bed, which Allie slept on. I made a bed for myself on the bench seat. My dad turned the light off and slid the accordion bedroom door shut. I glanced at Allie. "*Allie!*" I whispered. No answer. She had either fallen asleep immediately or was faking. I admired the moonlit sky through the window screen. The stars shone extra bright in this middle of nowhere. I felt tiny, almost suspended in them from my position on earth. I closed my eyes.

When I opened them, it was 5:45 a.m. The yellowed overhead light flicked on and whatever skin exposed from under our sheets looked mustard from its oily glaze. Allie rolled over and sucked in a yawn.

"It's time to get up. Rise and shine," Dad announced, rolling the accordion door back and digging through cabinets for things.

We rustled to our feet, pulling on our pants and T-shirts. The air was cold and damp, hanging on our forearms. We brushed our teeth, laced up our shoes, and stumbled down the hydraulic steps until we stood in a wet grass patch looking up at the open door. Dew drops shimmered on the saturated turf, mirroring the stars from the waning night sky. An eggshell blue morning warped overhead. Dad joined us outside. His hands moved confidently, clicking open metal doors of compartments nestled between the RV wheels, extracting first blue tarps and then large plastic crates.

"Let's go," he said, jerking the tarps at me.

I stepped forward and he dropped them in my outstretched arms that buckled like dry spaghetti noodles.

"Take those over to lot 312."

My preteen constitution miserably disagreed, but I followed orders because not following orders was not an option.

We unloaded the underbelly of the RV, falling into an assembly line cycle, transporting crates of costume jewelry over to our rented tent plot. The sky melted into golden tones as we worked together securing one tent pole into another, creating the frame for the booth, and draping tarps appropriately overhead. We unfolded tables and removed lids on plastic tubs. We revealed velvet pads, housing rows of silver and gold rings, from within those tubs, and arranged them on the tables.

Customers drifted past our booth at 7:15 a.m. like supernatural specters born from the morning mist. Dad became noticeably stressed, feverishly securing knock-off handbags from his set of plastic bins onto hooks attached to a metal grid he'd secured at the back wall of the booth. "Hurry up! We don't want to be setting up when it gets busy."

By 9:30 a.m. droves of people in sun hats, T-shirts, and jeans kicked up plumes of dust from the white gravel aisles with their sandals. Droplets of sweat skirted over my temples. Allie and I slumped lifelessly behind the table, blanketed by shade from the overhead tarp. My dad moved from one side of the booth to the other, clasping necklaces, answering questions. Then he turned and pulled a thick wad of cash from the tight back pocket of his jeans. He flicked a fat thumb through the bills, counting each one, and gestured to me with the wad.

"Here," he said. He peeled off twenty one-dollar bills, folded them in half over his index finger, and handed them to me, looking away. "Use this to make change. Don't lose it." I stuffed the bills into my own crinkled jean pocket.

I didn't know if it was the heat or if because Shipshewana was unpierceable by cell signal. Or if it were the unbearable sameness of the surrounding landscape. But Shipshewana gripped the existential dread at my center and yanked its beautiful and frightening weave to the forefront. The monotony of Shipshewana weekends was purgatorial, mooring me to my own humanity in a way that can only occur when we are suspended from distraction.

Doubly, I was confused by Amish culture. While I assumed the Amish didn't use technology, I was only partially right. The Amish Ordnung, an unwritten set of general Amish rules, does prohibit the use of public electricity.[13] However, I saw child after child in tattered linen pants rolled to their ankles, forsaking the luxury of shoes, walking the aisles unflinchingly barefoot, with their noses glued to brand-new Game Boy consoles. Their fingers punched the electronic buttons in the sun. *What's the point?*

The crowd slowed and I sat back on an empty crate. Dad sidled beside me, leaning against a tent pole in a contrapposto stance. We people watched. He jabbed my shoulder and then pointed at the felt tray of rings on the table.

"You see those?" he asked "You've gotta keep an eye on those. People steal rings." He wiped his nose with his thumb and switched his weight to his other hip. "They like to pick them up to try them on, which is fine, but sometimes when you're not looking, they'll slip one into their pocket."

After that, whenever people approached the rings, I monitored their fingers vigilantly. I hovered near them with an intensified presence. Though I never caught anyone, which either meant I was very skilled or very poor at my job.

We attended the Shipshewana market with my dad multiple weekends that summer and again during following summers. The days in the tent were long, and hours passed into the afternoon uneventfully. I learned how to tell a counterfeit

13 "What Is the Amish Ordnung?" Amish America, accessed January 16, 2021.

Kate Spade bag from a real one by the stitching on the inside. I learned about the variance of gold and what to look for in 925 stamped sterling silver, versus silver-coated metals.

If Allie and I were lucky, the tent across from ours was rented by a lean, young man in his twenties with hair gelled into pointy, frosted tips. He was selling some sort of animated, plush snake toy, or maybe it was a worm, attached to a clear fishing line. The fishing line was tied to a small stick that allowed him to manipulate the worm. It floated through the air as if it were autonomous, wriggled in the gravel, or jumped through hoops by its own free will. Small crowds bottlenecked the aisles to watch.

I liked watching him too. I liked being near him. I concluded he must be special to garner so much attention. He was a mysterious figure; a true icon of prosperity and success. I made excuses to walk to the soda machine at the end of our aisle, dragging my feet loudly through the gravel as I passed his tent, hoping to be noticed.

Sometimes when it was slow, he walked over to our tent and made chitchat with my dad. He had a nervous and eager disposition. I shrunk in his presence, never talked, only watched. In their conversations I heard my dad make broad, indisputable conclusions like "...as long as we break even," with his arms folded. I sensed these were negative because of how I read Dad's face, even though his tone meant to be expecting and confident.

After Frosted Tips returned to his own booth, Dad pulled a ham sandwich from the cooler. He peeled the cellophane from the damp bread, nodded in a general direction, and said "that guy's wife works around the corner in the 400's section." He took a bite from the sandwich. "A real sexy woman," he nodded, "a *knockout*. Blonde. Big breasts." He gestured to suggest the breasts of which he spoke. "She does really well for herself," he chewed. "They both do. They make a killing, but they work separately on purpose. She can't do business when he's around because she gets a lot of attention from the men. He works the women."

I could tell my father really admired this woman and that I should admire her too.

I scripted an itemized mental note of the elements that make a woman successful: *Blonde. Big breasts. Men.*

• • •

My dad, Allie, and I existed relatively nonconfrontationally while we were together in the booth: no speaking, just doing; side by side, preoccupied by a common goal. I bonded with him most when he wasn't trying to bond with me.

Whenever I did close a sale it was thrilling. I tried to contain the surge of excitement that flooded me behind stoic professionalism. When women tried on necklaces, I nervously passed the plastic hand mirror over the table, gold chains shimmering from their milky throats. "Do you have this in a fourteen-inch length?" they'd ask, rotating the tilted mirror around their busts. I ducked below the black table drapes and rummaged through the tubs until I found one.

I loved the feeling of cash in my hands. The filthier it was, the better. Its dirtiness made it respectable money—money that had *worked*, money with *clout*. I slipped the jewelry into a sealable plastic baggy and looked over to my father. He smiled at me, his daughter taking bumbling strides in passage to the American Dream.

5

HEAT

People have lots of names for the existential dread that I experienced in Shipshewana but I'll call it The Dread for short. All humans experience The Dread. For me, on the surface, it feels like urgent and generalized loneliness. Underneath, it reduces to despair over our imminent and inescapable end, garnished by a fear of panoramic meaninglessness.

The Dread is a fundamental part of being alive, and we have it because our consciousness exists only *within us*. No one can truly "know" us the way we know ourselves. The range of emotions and impulses we experience are far muddier and more complex than can be totally communicated through language. This is incredibly isolating, but also an extraordinary experience; to be so individual, but also so the same.

A wicked thin line divides The Dread and Presence. You can find that line in a Florida rainstorm.

When I was little, whenever it rained, I pulled an itchy quilt from the linen closet and spread it out on the concrete floor of the muggy garage. I rolled up the garage door halfway so that I could see the sky, but wouldn't get wet if rain blew in. Acoustic thunderclaps rippled threateningly, droplets shattered on the driveway, and leaves dragged in the opacity of the wind. Peering into the slate-colored atmosphere, unfailingly, The Dread appeared—a sensation of ultimate aloneness. But I didn't try to escape it. I laid on my stomach for hours and let it wash over me. I was The Dread and The Dread was me. Transcending, we were everything everywhere.

At some point, when I stopped practicing sitting with The Dread, The Dread became too much to bear. Instead, I tried to cheat The Dread, or solve The Dread, or flee The Dread. I thought I could hush The Dread with sex, or booze, or food. But when I juked to the left, it juked left too. Bettering my external circumstances with new jobs, friends, or living situations has been known to substantially ease the drumming resonation of The Dread. But The Dread remains forever nestled within me. It is one of many reckonings.

• • •

My curly hair was as thick, and coarse, and rebellious as Florida fauna—a special concoction of Italian genetics built durable to withstand unforgivable climates.

Sometimes people made the mistake of brushing it. One time at a sleepover, a friend's mother placed a chair in the center of the room. She was Pacific Asian and her hair was long and silky. One at a time, partygoers took the seat. She twisted each person's hair into even braids, or arranged it atop their crowns with pins and clips.

When it was my turn, she sunk the bristles of a wooden brush into my hair. Raking it through, the bristles snagged into the fibrous bulk. The brush was stuck. She jerked it downward to force it out and my entire head jerked with it, rocking me backward. Pain seared across my scalp. Everyone watched in silent horror. She pulled forcibly a second, third, and fourth time. The wooden brush burst into halves right down the center—one half in her hand, the other hanging from my head.

In early millennia, we were a Euro-centric, straight-hair worshipping nation. And we were expected to do anything within our power to meet this criteria held against us. There were little to no role models normalizing curly hair, and definitely not anyone celebrated strictly for their physical beauty. (Note: wavy hair doesn't count. I'm talking spirals the diameter of a marker or tighter). For ten years, from 2000 to 2010, all of the female identifying celebrities on *Forbes'* highest paid celebrities list rocked straight hair or blow outs, including (listed alphabetically): Jennifer Aniston, Fiona Armstrong, Beyoncé, Sandra Bullock, Mariah Carey, Cher, Celine Dion, Lady Gaga, Angelina Jolie, Jennifer Lopez, Madonna, Julia Roberts, J.K. Rowling, Britney Spears, and Oprah Winfrey.[14] Beyoncé is the stand out exception from the list, flaunting her natural hair the most.

The closest example I had to relate to as a child was a fake person: Hermione Granger from the *Harry Potter* series. Even her thick, textured hair was described in the novel as "bushy" and "messy," suggesting homeliness. I also had Scary Spice from the Spice Girls to look to. However, when assigned to pretend-play Scary Spice during dance parties with friends, it was out of mockery, not admiration. In an article published in the British magazine *Top of the Pops,* Journalist Peter Loraine dubbed member Melanie B, the only woman of color with voluminous, textured hair from the group of otherwise white musicians with straight hair, as "scary."[15] The nickname stuck, whether ill intended by Loraine or not.

---

14 "Forbes Lists," Forbes, accessed February 15, 2021.

15 Lauren Smith, "How the Spice Girls Really Got Their Names," Grazia, accessed September 09, 2015.

Maggie, who's mom bought her the most coveted hair straightener available, said things like "your hair looks prettier when it's wet" and "we would make the perfect person if we combined *my* looks with *your* brain."

Everywhere I looked, the world seemed to say, "What you are naturally is incorrect, and needs to be fixed. Big hair is bad. Wild hair is weird. Frizz is foe. Your hair should be controlled."

Eventually, I took mercy upon myself and began slicking it into low, tidy buns. Per request, my mom brought home enormous bottles of industrial hair gel from Walmart that only seemed to be manufactured in otherworldly colors, like electric yellow or glacial blue. Facing the bathroom mirror before school, I slopped the gel onto the top of my head and combed the hairs into a tight, low bundle above my shirt collar. Very eighteenth-century silversmith looking. Very Paul Revere. This look was manageable. This look was fine.

I wore it in gelled buns for so long, that it grew down to my waist. At age twelve, my older cousin showed me how to press it straight with a clothing iron. We took turns lying on our backs over a towel laid out beneath us on the carpet, hair splayed out behind us. One of us ran the clothing iron over the other one's hairs, flattening them out, then we swapped. I ran my fingers through its length from root to tip, swooning at its shininess, its easiness. This was intoxicating. I tucked it in and out from behind my ears, pushed my bangs backward and let them fall gracefully into my eyes. I braided my hair, pulled it up in ponytails, and turned my head from side to side to feel it's movement and body. My hair was suddenly simple, like I wanted to be too. I pleaded with my mother for a hair straightener of my own.

On Christmas morning, at thirteen years old, I got my wish. I tore the device from its packaging. I couldn't wait to plug it into the wall and to use its white-hot energy to deliver me from the misery of my otherness.

I wore my hair straight to school every single day after that, like all of my peers, and all of our idols. I worked *intensively* to blend in, developing calluses on my palms from the hours of heat boring through the plastic handles. If the weather was above thirty percent humidity outside—and it was often up to ninety—I wore a sweatshirt to school with the hood pulled over my head. I refused to pull it down until I was inside a climate-controlled building.

The belief that only straight hair was lovable was further qualified when I was rewarded positively for my efforts. My change in appearance intersected exactly with my first boyfriend.

The truth is that faking it *works*. But it will undoubtedly cost you.

• • •

I met Daniel in seventh period of the eighth grade. On the last day of the school year, he asked me to be his girlfriend. We arranged to meet at the movies over the weekend for our first date. I was too scared to go alone, so I invited Maggie to chaperone. He invited some of his friends too.

Saturday evening, I sat in the back seat of Maggie's mom's Rolls Royce and Maggie and her mother sat in the front. Daniel had assured me he'd be waiting out in front of the theater at 5:30 p.m. To say I was nervous would be an understatement. The aspirations of my perfectionism, my impulses to control the situation, to be liked and desired by both my friend and my new boyfriend were all consuming.

The Rolls Royce barreled down the highway, headed into town, and my hands started to sweat. One of my legs bounced in place, shaking my whole body. Pine trees coagulated into a blur beyond the window. I wrapped a finger around a straightened lock of hair and twirled it in a spiral, something I was increasingly doing when I felt anxious. I looked down to examine the lock, running the hair between my fingertips. I noticed frail spots and split ends from heat damage. I gently placed my thumb and forefinger together, pinched the tip of a damaged strand, and pulled. The tip broke off from the weak spot. Relief.

I sifted through the hairs with laser-focused precision, isolated another one with heat damage, and pulled at its tip until it snapped. Concentrating on this minor thing lulled me into a stupor. My leg still shook but I didn't feel it anymore. I didn't feel anything. All of my bodily sensations soothed into a solitary sensation of calm.

We turned off the highway exit ramp and I came to. I looked down and little, golden hair fragments littered my white polo shirt over my breast. A surge of shame and fear. *What have I done?* I glanced at the back of Maggie's head, then at her mom's, and dusted off the hairs discreetly. We pulled into the movie theater parking lot. Far away, I spotted Daniel and his two friends leaning against the cement pillars in front of the ticket booth.

I gave my shirt a final glance to be sure evidence of the pulling was gone and my appearance was tidy. Confirmed: I was spotless.

• • •

I dated Daniel for two years into high school. When I turned fifteen in my sophomore year, my parents made me get a job. I worked as a cashier at a grocery store chain located a mile down the road from our house. There, I met a boy named Ben who was three years older than me. I developed a crush on him.

All the times I was made aware by Daniel, or others, that I was hurting him with my shady behavior, or by ignoring his phone calls, I didn't feel sadness or sympathy, I felt rage. I was falling out of my first love, even though I didn't want to be, and I was frustrated by the loss of control. *I* didn't even like *my own* behavior, and this made me even angrier. Conversely, I also felt entitled to my heart's demands: Ben.

Instead of managing my relationship with Daniel, I ignored it. While Daniel was away for a summer, Ben came over to my house to watch a movie with me and Maggie. I kissed him in the foyer before walking him out to his car at the end of the night. I broke up with Daniel the following day over the phone. Daniel cried into the receiver and I cried too. I punished myself for months afterward. I felt irresponsible, negligent, and dangerous. I was scared of how my love, or the withdrawal of it, could hurt myself and others so deeply. Instead of letting Daniel have some space to heal, I drew him even closer.

Daniel continued calling every night, even though I was seeing Ben. I feared if he pulled away completely, The Dread would become uncorked, burst into a torrent through the opening Daniel previously inhabited, and end me. I desperately needed Daniel's attention *and* Ben's attention to neatly occupy all of my empty feeling spaces—to seal me in an airtight vacuum so I did not have to experience any of the pain that had accumulated in the making of my life so far.

• • •

After Daniel and I broke up, I became a drifter at school. Ben had already graduated high school, my friends from work went to a different school than me, and my friendship with Maggie was falling out.

Lunch period was particularly tough. I liked to think of myself as an outlaw, proudly roaming sunset plains on a mustang, sure of myself and my solitude. Except I was trapped within the walls of my high school campus, and my mustang was a toilet in the women's restroom where I sat to pass time. Sometimes I took refuge in an empty classroom and read books. If I walked around aimlessly, I made it look intentional, like I had somewhere to be. Humiliated by this lack of belonging, I just needed to keep moving. Movement seemed purposeful.

In my junior year, I discovered a deep comfort in my art classes. Because I enjoyed the work and was skilled at it, I didn't feel pressured to prove I belonged there. This inherent belonging was a type of magic that drew cohesive friendships to me. I bonded with friends I met in art class who were intellectual, absurd, and funny—like me. These new friends cared about things, and they were held down to earth by academic attachments like Yearbook club, tennis practices, and cross-country running. We experimented with drugs and alcohol on the weekends, but not in the ways I had previously done with Maggie, which was becoming sinister.

One day, I opened the door to the art room to eat lunch with my new friends, but the room was empty. I took a walk to the courtyard and discovered them lounging around a circular metal table in the sun. Some kids I didn't recognize hovered in the vicinity. I felt a pang of insecurity, but smiled and waved as I approached.

There was an empty seat at the table. "Hey!" I said. "Can I sit here with you all?"

"Of course!" they answered, and I squeezed in.

Noon and eighty degrees outside, I'd braided my hair back that morning to keep it off my neck. From three years of straightening, and chemical keratin treatments, my hair was becoming brittle. I'd cropped it from my waist to the middle of my back, and finally to my shoulders because the ends were crispier than a fourth of July funnel cake.

The hair near the nape of my neck was especially textured and whenever The Dread broke over me, I reflexively located my hands to that site. When I ran my fingertips over it—felt its bumpiness—my animal intuition said *pull*. So I did. When the hairs broke midway along the shaft, I felt inexplicably soothed. I knew the continuous pulling was potentially damaging to my scalp, but the sensation it provided was irresistible. The act could be compared to the relief from scratching an itchy mosquito bite, though the scratching may cause the skin to break and bleed.

I was deeply ashamed and afraid of my impulses to pull and I disguised the aftermath of the pulling as much as possible. Visibly broken and shorter than the hairs around them, I pinned back the sections near my neck with bobby pins, stuffing them covertly into my braids. Throughout the transitions of the day, they must've come loose.

I pulled a sandwich from my bag, removed its plastic container, and peeled away the crusts. As I dropped the ribbon of crust onto the metal table, a girl to my left, who I was not acquainted with, turned to look at me and did not stop looking. I raised the sandwich to my mouth, bit down, and she boldly asked "Why does your hair look like that?"

Everyone hushed and fixed their attention on us. Doubtless that her question was super charged, perforating me with the electric current of one billion joules, I was surely going to die by the electrocution of this embarrassment, no less with my mouth full of deli meat. I chewed and chewed, but my throat constricted to a pinhole. Swallowing the sandwich bite felt like forcing a cantaloupe through a straw.

"What do you mean?" I asked uneasily with my mouth full.

"There," she said, and pointed at the back of my neck. "The hair there is way shorter than everywhere else. Did you cut it like that on purpose?"

She stared at me blankly and I dared not turn my head to the faces trained on us. I struggled to formulate an answer. I didn't know why I did what I did.

"Is it?" I stammered.

"Yeah!" she said enthusiastically, grabbing a braid and lifting it, examining the hair underneath. "Actually, it looks more like it's breaking off."

"*Weird,*" I replied over my chewing. "Maybe from tying it back too tightly or something."

"Yeah," she said, releasing the braid and furrowing her brow. She dropped the subject, but I sensed an internal processing happening behind her eyes. Everyone went back to their conversations. I went back to my sandwich.

6

PANTHERS

When I was six years old, the Florida Fish and Wildlife Conservation Commission released twenty panthers into the jungles surrounding our house. The Florida panthers were endangered, but I wasn't focused on the details of why they were released, as much as the potential aftermath. I imagined them at night while falling asleep. I dreamt of them bursting through my bedroom window, glass shattering, claws bared, snarling, and eager to attack.

My bedroom was at the front of the house, clear of bushes or obstruction. Naturally, if the panthers felt called to rampage, my bedroom would be the likely place they would start. I abandoned my bedroom frequently to sleep in Allie's down the hall because she had bunk beds. I waited until the house went dark, climbed out of my bed, and crept past the glow of the night light. I climbed the iron rungs to the bunk above hers and slithered under the top sheet, pulling the covers up to my chin. My face was a foot from the ceiling, but I preferred the squatness of this space. I felt safe in Allie's room toward the back of the house, protected, my body stacked above hers in a perfect line.

By middle school, Allie and I were dislocated, shifting in opposite directions and gathering speed. Here and there were flashes of playfulness, when she held me down and tickled me until I gasped for air, but hostility was baked into most exchanges.

We both needed nurturing. Although Allie may have needed even more specialized attention as, not only was she contextualizing herself in the world like me, but was also contextualizing herself in our family as an adopted person. Our desperate need for care calls to my mind the Roman sculpture Lupa Capitolina, by Antonio del Pollaiuolo. The sculpture depicts two infants, Romulus and Remus, suckling from the breast of a she-wolf, which saved the twins from their abandonment into a raging river.[16]

However, Allie and I didn't have a supernatural, lactating she-wolf at the ready for our savior. We had our human mother who was recovering from domestic abuse, working forty hours a week, and taking night classes to get her Bachelor of Science in Nursing. Economically, Allie and my individual demands for attention outweighed the supply Mom was able to provide, which raised the price for it. According to the rules of natural selection, Allie and I were pit against each other in competition.

Our strategies for getting love developed differently. Allie was outspoken, charming, and pushy. When she desired something—clothes, toys, a later curfew, money—she relentlessly badgered or guilt tripped until Mom gave in. If all else failed, she threw a Hail Mary and used the fact that she was adopted as the bottom line.

This strategy worked, so she repeated it. I perceived Allie's pressuring as manipulative and having a taxing effect on

---

16 *Ancient History Encyclopedia*, s.v. "Romulus and Remus," by Brittany Garcia, published April, 18, 2018.

Mom, who was visibly exasperated. It frightened me. Our mother was the twine tenuously securing our family unit. If I detected fraying at the seams, I became protective of our mother, and thus of us as a family.

I resented Allie for her insistence and desires. Allie's outright sense of deservingness was antithetic to my lack thereof. So, to offset her, I asked for nothing. A martyr, I withdrew from my needs in totality, folding myself into a quiet, unobtrusive stone.

• • •

While Allie was well versed in the art of accessorizing, I found makeup intriguing, but I didn't feel it was available to me. An invisible representative was pressing me to choose between two costumes: one that was pink or one that was blue, bedazzled or bland, tight or loose.

I was confused. I wanted to tromp the backwoods of our neighborhood in hiking boots, searching for cottonmouth snakes, but also flaunt two-piece swimsuits. I longed to glitter like an iridescent chandelier, but also comb the muddy creek beds for arrowheads. I skimmed articles on dinosaurs from *Discovery Kids*, but wished to scour the pages of *Seventeen Magazine* with my sullied fingernails. I hungered for the magic, illusion, and fantasy that makeup could provide, but this cross-pollinated profile of a person, hybridizing the masculine and feminine, had not been green-lit by the masses and rolled out as an option for normal people yet. In my heart was the flare of David Bowie, but in the streets, I committed to the usual: blue, bland, loose.

The first time I did experiment with makeup, I snuck into my mother's bathroom and stole an eyeliner pencil from her drawer. I smuggled the pencil beneath the waistband of my jeans across the house, into my bedroom, locking the door behind me. Alone, I propped a plastic, purple hand mirror on my dresser and gazed into it. I uncapped the pencil, steadied my hand, and dragged a black line from the clay tip over my almond shaped eyelid—how I'd seen in *Cosmopolitan* Magazine. I bat my lashes and tilted my face from side to side. *Need better lighting.*

As soon as I stepped into the hallway, Allie's door flew open. She and a friend stood opposite, staring blankly. Their eyes cast from my face to the pencil in my hand. They grinned devilishly, then sounded alarm. "Makeup! Makeup! You're wearing makeup!" They yelled. I stepped around them into the bathroom and slammed the door. They banged on it. "Let us see!" they squealed from the other side. When I opened the door, I stood plainly with my arms at my sides, vulnerable as ever, allowing them to examine my eyelids like a quality control inspection. Allie leaned in closely. Then she took a step back and put her hands on her hips. "Well," she said. "It's about time. Everyone at school thinks you're a lesbian."

• • •

When I was twelve and Allie was thirteen, our mom walked in on Allie having sex with her boyfriend. When Mom shared this experience with me during one of our car rides to basketball practice, I was outraged. When passing Allie in the hall for the next few days, I couldn't even look at her.

How could she do that to her body? I asked myself righteously, lying flat on my purple bedspread. *How could she give herself over like that?* From the perch of my own adolescence, I considered how young we both were, how we still played like children, spit water through foam pool noodles, sucked Cheeto dust from our fingers, and chugged full glasses of milk. As less than twenty percent of adolescents report having sex before the age of fifteen, I didn't know anyone our age who'd had sex.[17] Sex felt so *adult*.

The intensity of my scorn confused me. On one hand, I was jealous. She'd stepped over a threshold I could only squint past. All I had were my desires for lovability. She had actualization. On the other hand, this newfound superiority distanced her even further from me, causing me to mourn our separateness. Her maturity made her untouchable.

As her peer, I held her decision to have sex in contempt. As an adult looking back, I interpret it as a bid for love. The sex wasn't about sex at all, it was about acceptance and security seeking. Ironically, my outrage illuminated how highly I regarded Allie. It reflected how I wanted her to see herself—as I saw her—which was invaluable.

• • •

Through middle school into high school, the more popular Allie became, the more caustic the music she listened to, the more she snuck out of her bedroom at night, skipped school, came home wasted, did drugs, and lashed out, at times becoming physically violent. At school, older boys I didn't know hovered over me in corridors and asked if I wanted to know what everyone saw my sister do to them in the back seat of their cars last weekend.

My parents exhaustively pivoted to ebb her momentum, and Allie bucked against them. They imposed special curfews, brought therapists into our home, and sent her to institutionalized sleepaway camps. Mom was convinced her friends were the cause of her erratic behavior so she enrolled Allie into a

---

17 Guttmacher Institute, "Adolescent Sexual and Reproductive Health," Figure 1.

different high school across town. However, because Allie's car privileges were suspended, she had no way of getting there. The new school wasn't too far from where Mom worked, so Mom outfit a bed for Allie in the back of her car and took Allie to work with her each morning at five o'clock. Allie slept in the trunk until Mom's fifteen-minute break at 8:00 a.m. when Mom ran out to her car, sped Allie to her new school, and dropped her off before her first class.

My parent's preoccupation with Allie incidentally left me in charge of raising myself. Mom rewarded and supported my academic achievements in her periphery. For years, on car rides to and from practices or events, she vented at length to me about what Allie had done wrong that week, who's house she'd slept at without asking, what lighters, weed, or cigarettes she'd found in the pockets of Allie's jeans. The conversation was always slanted toward Allie.

"How's school?" Mom asked from the driver's seat.

"Good," I mumbled.

Unfazed by my brevity, "Allie is making me crazy. I found an open bottle of Jack Daniels in the back seat of her car Saturday night. And when she walked in the door, she smelled like a bar. Maybe I should just take back all the gifts I've already bought her for Christmas this year and wrap up packs of cigarettes. What do you think?"

I learned that if I needed emotional support for a problem I was having, there was no space leftover in my household. I would have to outsource it to my friends at school. To air my problems in my home would add to the mounting load of turmoil already ensuing. My role was to restore order and peace by being an easy perfectionist, counterpoising chaos by listening quietly. Leveling the scale, the worse Allie was, the better I had to be.

That didn't mean I wasn't unraveling too; I'd just learned from Allie's mistakes. I guzzled down sixteen-ounce cans of Natural Light poured into a thermos each morning on the drive to school. At 7:00 a.m. I was drunk through first period, but passed my advanced placement courses with A's and B's. I ripped my hairs out strand by strand, but competed and placed in statewide art competitions. I was addicted and codependent on my boyfriends, but racing in cross-country meets. I was a high-functioning mess. I unraveled with finesse.

• • •

Physical altercations normalized between Allie and me. We were keyed up like Florida panthers scrapping for meat. Spats over petty things transformed rapidly and catastrophically, resembling WWE worthy brawls.

After school one day, while pouring a cup of juice in the kitchen, she took the first swing.

"You know that's not really healthy right?" she said eyeing the cup from the other side of the counter. "It's actually filled with chemicals and sugar. It's probably going to give you cancer."

I scowled at her as it streamed into the glass. "It's orange juice. It's fine."

I sipped the juice, clearing the glass, stood from the table, and placed the cup in the sink. As I exited into the living room, she shoulder checked me. I turned and shoved her. "Don't touch me!" I growled. She tackled me to the ground and we wrestled on the living room rug, knocking into furniture.

She planted herself on my back and pinned my arms to the ground with her knees. Then wrapped her fingers around the back of my head and smashed my face into the carpet fibers. The friction from writhing under her weight left burns on my elbows. In our jostling, a remote control toppled from the couch arm onto the floor.

When she released me, I was panting, hair a mess, face down. She smugly rose to her feet and swaggered toward her bedroom. I lifted my red, carpet-burned face from the floor, propped myself onto one elbow, and reached for the remote control. I cocked back and whipped it at the back of her head as hard as I could. It cracked against her shoulder-blade and she fell forward into the wall, crying out.

There came a day soon after that, while we were still enrolled in the same high school, when my mother asked Allie to drive me to school with her. My car was in the shop and I'd already missed the bus. "Fine," said Allie. When it was time to leave, I settled into her passenger seat, which was tilted fully horizontal. Turning the key, the subwoofers behind my head blasted at an amplification that rattled my seat.

Still dark outside, she reversed out of the driveway, whipped into drive, and zoomed out of the neighborhood toward the interstate. I made a show of clicking my seat belt pretentiously into its receiver. Allie turned up the already blasting music a touch louder. Retorting, I raised my hand slowly and quietly from my lap toward my forehead. Allie's eyes darted over to me. Indiscreetly, I made the sign of the cross; a notch at my forehead, chest, and above either breast.

She rolled her eyes and grunted in disgust. "You're so *annoying*!" I was.

"No, I'm not! Your driving is scary!" It was.

We thundered across the overpass, down the other side, and swung onto the merge ramp.

"You're such a little bitch!" she snarled. "You're lucky I even let you in my car."

My hands trembled as we accelerated to merge. "Fuck you!" I shouted hoarsely. "You think I want to be here with you? I fucking hate you!"

At forty miles per hour, she slammed on the brakes. The inertia sent loose items—our backpacks, pens, pennies, gum wrappers, beads slung around the rearview mirror—crashing into the windshield. My body launched forward into the seat belt, which locked, cutting into my chest. I detected a loud ringing, then realized it was coming from my mouth. I was screaming. Parked in the center of the on-ramp, Allie's expression was rendered in fury. She lunged at me, wrapping her fingers in my tousled hair and jerked me by the head. Like a doll, my body folded over the center console, head into her lap. Her fists wailed on my skull.

Trapped in place by the seat belt, I scrambled like a feral animal beneath the pounding. When I broke free, I threw open the door and snatched my bag from the floor. Toppling onto the road shoulder, I slammed the door behind me and stumbled toward the bridge. Daylight was breaking. My eyebrow was bleeding.

She threw the car into reverse and annunciated through the open passenger side window "Get in."

I ignored her.

"Get. In."

Finally, the car lurched into drive and sped off. I observed from the rumble strips as she executed a nearly perfect merge into the middle lane of the interstate.

• • •

Our shared history was the sediment indisputably connecting me and Allie, but also thwarting us when we weaponized it. Sharpening spears, we workshopped our language over many years, pointing our insults at each other's secret weak spots with vicious specificity.

However, my position as the biological child lent me a degree of immunity that neither of us quite understood with our minds but felt in our hearts. Despite that Allie exploited her adoption story to get what she wanted, her origins as the adopted kid haunted her; caused her to feel inherently alien and separate from our family. While I sensed this, I didn't do anything to help. At times I even amplified it as a short-term defense to disarm her if she was attacking me. As a long-term pattern, it splintered her personhood.

• • •

I hated Allie, but I also loved Allie. I deeply wanted her to think I was cool. I didn't care to infiltrate her world, her friendships, or even to be like her. I wanted her to be *her*, and me to be *me*, and to share closeness despite our differences. The more concentrated this desire became, the more pain I felt when it was rejected.

Though, I believe Allie felt the same. Even though the bigness of our complexities overwhelmed us, we shared an unwavering alliance below the surface. If shit were to ever hit the fan, if I ever called her in distress, I knew she would be there in some capacity.

Our alliance exposed itself in protective flickers. Like when an older boy stole a hairbrush from my backpack in the sixth grade, and brandished it to the children in the seats behind me. "Look!" he shouted, pretending to brush his hair in exaggerated motions. He inserted his face in between the leather seat and the window and whispered into my ear "you're *ugly*."

I fixed my gaze through the window, frozen, pretending not to notice as kids snickered in the surrounding seats, glancing back and forth between him and me. The warmth of humiliation crept over my face. When Allie noticed what was happening, she hurled herself over the seat and tugged the hairbrush out of the boy's hand. "Shut up, Alex!" she lashed at him, and tossed the hairbrush back to me.

When everyone was facing forward again, when order was restored, she propped herself high above the masses, and announced proudly "That's right! Nobody picks on my little sister, except for me."

PART TWO

7

CHEMISTRY

I applied to a few different state universities. Florida State was my first choice, but when admission letters rolled into mailboxes across the county mine said I was wait listed. I could have waited on standby in case a spot opened up for me, but I didn't want to take the risk. I accepted an admissions letter to a smaller, coastal school called the University of North Florida. They didn't have a football team, but they did have a beach.

I arrived to college in August, nervous but excited by the possibilities newness could bring. No one knew me as "Allie's little sister." No one knew me at all.

I'd been dating Ben for over two years. I probably could've made my relationship with him work, despite the hour and a half distance between us, if it weren't for this thing about me, which he knew: I really liked to drink. Drinking *made sense* of me.

My first week on campus I made friends with some people who lived in my dorm. That weekend, three of us hung out in someone's dorm room who provided a fifty-two-ounce bottle of rum. We cleared the bottle in two hours, and I passed out in my dorm-room bathroom and shit my pants. My roommate, a chaste, Christian woman who'd never consumed a drop of alcohol in her life, found me lying on the tile floor covered in my own refuse. She wanted to call an ambulance for fear that I'd overdosed, but some girls down the hall, who would soon become my best friends, helped her clean me off in the shower, give me Gatorade, and lift me into my bed.

Up to that point, all the stress and fear I'd experienced, my trauma and neglect, was a mounting turbulence that I'd slopped under my surface self. I'd thought if I crammed it or numbed it, I eliminated the risk, or so I believed, of hurting—or worse, *losing*—the people I loved with my truths. But it was starting to spill out.

These bad feelings were less a solid state, able to be crated and stowed away, than they were liquid, unexpressed energy. Liquid keeps its volume, but takes on the shape of its container. So when I shoved down my trauma by ignoring it, it simply shifted elsewhere, migrating toward any punctures at the surface. Pulling at my split ends released it in spritzes, but alcohol brought everything boiling to the top. When I was wasted, finally, *finally,* my outsides reflected my insides.

The National Institute of Health equates binge drinking for female bodies to four or more drinks over two hours.[18] For a stretch of two months, I consumed thirteen beers every night. At the club on the weekends, I downed five shots of tequila, a beer in between, then a Red Bull energy drink. I danced to music booming so loudly it rattled my skeleton. I purged everything into the toilet by daybreak. The following morning, I was fresh as a daisy.

---

18 "Alcohol's Effects on Health: College Drinking," National Institute on Alcohol Abuse and Alcoholism, updated January 2021.

Ben and my relationship lasted four months into the school year. Our last night as a couple I fumed at him through the phone. My butt cheeks were nearly visible beneath the seams of a short dress, as I stomped around my dorm room. My new friends did their makeup in the mirror over my bathroom sink.

"I have to go," I shouted over a hairdryer. "Everyone is waiting on me."

"Who is 'everyone'?" he asked. "Who even are you anymore? You're just some drunk club girl at the bars every night. I don't even know you."

My new friends became my best friends because they kept me at a safe distance from my feelings, which I liked and encouraged. After Ben and I broke up, if I happened to catch a glimpse of my dejected reflection in the mirror, my new friends rushed into my dorm room and pulled me into the bathroom to take bong rips. They were reverse bodyguards, buffering me from the discomfort of my needs. I stayed so high after the breakup that I blacked out two whole weeks. The memory of my breakup is nothing. A dumb void.

I was too habitually hungover to attend my 9:00 a.m. Statistics course for three weeks. I was failing three out of four classes. I had never failed a class in my life. Without a predesigned structure that someone else composed for me, I was falling apart. I didn't know how to hold myself upright when it was such a *relief* to become unraveled.

I visited my family in Ormond Beach less and less. When I did make the drive, I consistently promised to show up by noon, but pulled in the driveway at 5:00 p.m. I walked directly to my bedroom, closed the door, and slept. I noticed my mom began leaving small clippings from the health section of the newspaper on my dresser. The titles read something like “The Dangers of Binge Drinking.” When I woke from my naps at 8:00 p.m., I’d crumple the clippings into a ball in my fist, carry them into the kitchen, and toss them spitefully into the trash in front of her.

In December, grades were distributed for the first semester. I somehow managed to pass three of my classes, even with nightclub stamps reading “under 21” smeared on the backs of my hands. I failed Earth Science and would need to take it again the following semester. Later that day, I got a call from my mother. Allie was pregnant. She was growing a baby girl inside of her. A tiny, little house on fire.

• • •

I spent the winter holiday at home with my parents, but Allie never came by. In the spring, I partied with my new friends even more than before. For the first time since I was thirteen years old, I was single and unsure of what to do with myself. I tried to remedy this by finding something to reattach to. I flirted with several people at once, took down phone numbers here and there, kissed and held hands with strangers at parties.

Unexpectedly, while attending a friend’s soccer game, I took a unique liking to someone that I recognized from the dorms. He noticed me too and waved me over. We sat beside each other and chatted over the hour. He had to leave the game early, so we said a friendly goodbye and he excused himself. I didn’t feel exceptionally drawn to him during the game, but when he stood up to leave, unlatched his bike from the dock down below, and swung his leg over it, something came over me.

I stood up from the top of the bleachers and shouted, before an audience, “Hey Aaron!”

He turned and looked.

“Nice ass!”

• • •

I dated Aaron for a total of two years. My past boyfriends were kind and chivalrous to me, but Aaron was different. I mistook his meanness for authenticity. I was obsessed with the concept of being real.

A second-choice school for both of us, an "out of place" feeling became our cohesion, and we clung to one another. The relationship was stormy, but when we weren't arguing we sprawled in the grass in between classes, dragging our index fingers over glossy pictures in my art books. We listened to records in his dorm room, sipped from huge bottles of white wine in bed, and shared secrets.

Aaron was the only person I confessed to about my hair pulling. Alone in my dorm room with the lights turned down, we passed a wine bottle back and forth while I sketched his likeness with charcoal sticks for my drawing class. I took a break and set the charcoal and notebook in my lap.

"Why do you do that?" He asked.

"Do what?"

"That," he said, nodding at my fingers pinching a lock of hair.

I froze. "I don't know. Stress, I think."

"Do you pull it out?" he asked, seriously.

I was fully dressed, but felt exposed, like being drawn from my own skin. "Sometimes."

He looked blankly at me.

"I guess when I'm stressed I do this, but sometimes I don't even realize it. I zone out. It's a nervous habit."

"You're neurotic," he said, taking a swig from the bottle.

I was paralytic. I braced for him to run out of the room shrieking or gagging. To call me a freak, break up with me, or change the subject. But then he relaxed and casually said "I have a friend who does that too."

I inhaled. "You do?"

"Yeah. My best friend Kelly. I've known her since I was six. She pulls out her eyebrows. She's a quiet, sensitive person. Super introverted. When she gets really anxious, she runs her fingers over her eyebrow hairs and plucks them out." He demonstrated. "Sometimes her eyelashes too. One time she pulled out *all* the eyelashes on one of her eyelids. She showed me. She said it feels good."

He passed the wine bottle to me.

I slumped back against the concrete wall. "Oh. Huh," I grunted. "I have done that too. Not pulled all of my eyelashes out, but I understand what she means. It does feel good. It's weird."

"I don't get it," he said, tugging at his eyelashes. "It just hurts for me."

We giggled and I rested my head on his shoulder. We changed the subject.

So easily, I was seen, spared from an anvil of shame. He'd sat with me in my truth, and met it with humor, empathy, and understanding. That felt like love.

• • •

Sharing interests with a romantic partner wasn't just refreshing, it was exhilarating. Rare and electric. Aaron added to conversations I cared to have. He showed me new music, literature, and artists I'd not yet known. In our common studies, I redefined what I understood as "beauty." I edged away from the religion I was raised in and moved toward science—stars, nebulas, galaxies, and quasars—ideologies that felt more heavenly to me.

We partied well together, binging on alcohol and academia, alternating between drinking until we went cross-eyed and studying until 3:00 a.m. When I started tipping too far over the edge to manage my responsibilities, he let me know—albeit unpleasantly. My roommates suggested between our arguments that he was controlling, but I secretly depended on our spats, about with who and how much I drank, because they kept me anchored to something.

This all, however, came at a price. As the relationship progressed, Aaron reminded me my appearance, and therefore value, reflected his appearance and value too. If I wore a sweatshirt to a party that he deemed uncool, he pulled me aside and pressured me to change it. When he introduced me to some friends back home, and they laid around chain smoking cigarettes indoors while watching reruns of *Breaking Bad* from dawn until dusk, he was annoyed with me for looking restless and out of place.

So I changed my sweatshirts and I smoked more cigarettes. I made these adjustments as monthly payments for all the beauty he was willing to unveil to me. I was on the hook for the expansive feelings manufactured by him. Paired with his influence, The Dread was insidious. I never paused to consider my own value—there was *no time*. I stayed urgently scared of my loneliness and of losing him, especially when I found text messages to exes in his phone down the line. I was *extra lucky* to be chosen by him as the sole receiver of his charms. It *made sense* to fight for him, to change myself because *who was I without him?*

When he transferred to his first-choice school, which was also my first-choice school, he asked me to follow him. I considered applying to the Bachelor of Fine Arts program at Florida State University, and I probably would've gotten in, but something in my gut held me in place. I rejected the narrative of abandoning my life to follow a man, even if it was in the direction of something I wanted. The idea of chasing him made me feel prickly underneath. I wanted the actualization of my desires to be on my own terms. I wanted ownership over my story. So I stayed.

The pain I felt when he left was unbearable. He visited many times during the following year, though always under the guise of seeing our mutual friends. He stayed at my house all weekend, told me he loved me, then ignored me for months, until visiting again. This was a pattern I was comfortable with, one not so unparalleled with my father. The chemical high I felt from Aaron's occasional closeness was thrilling. As with alcohol, all my suppressed feelings came forward and I conflated this surge of hormones for love. I discarded myself in his wake again and again, committed to the addiction of these weekend highs. He was the most unique lover in the entire world, and he confirmed this for me when we broke up for good.

I made a phone call midway through my junior year that haunted me for a decade. I dialed his number while pacing behind a Jiffy Lube, waiting on an oil change. When he answered the phone, I sobbed. Snot dripped down the front of my shirt. "I'm sorry," I wept, "but you can't stay with me anymore when you come into town. I have a new boyfriend. This is over." This was true. I did have a new boyfriend—one I didn't much care for because he was an alcoholic, like me—but I needed something to throw in front of myself. I couldn't break the cycle of us on my own, and Aaron certainly had no plans to.

To this, he was steel.

"Cool," he said, coldly. "No problem."

"I'm so sorry, Aaron," I breathed. "This is so painful."

"I'm not worried about it." His end of the line was quiet, but I heard him fiddling with something, like a jacket zipper. "I hope this new guy treats you well. But I think you should know, for your own sake, you'll never find *anyone* like me."

• • •

My binge drinking advanced.

The summer after my junior year, my mom drove me to the Jacksonville airport. I pooled into the group of students waiting at the gate to board a plane to Rome, Italy. The study abroad trip she had encouraged me to take was a month long with a focused itinerary for Fine Arts majors. I'd never been out of the country before, except for a few touristy cruises as a kid to Mexico or the Bahamas. I didn't know what to expect.

When I arrived at the dormitories on Saint John's University International campus, I quickly realized that I was split between cliques. I didn't fit in with the wealthy, popular group. I certainly didn't match the prim, studious types, who were married and in bed by 9:00 p.m. I didn't feel quite right within the small band of social floaters, even though that's what I turned out to be.

I was friendly with everyone, but I spent my free time during the days alone. Newness and ignorance shielded me from fear as I zigzagged across the city on foot. I carried my sketchbook in my backpack and let myself be lost, feeling charmed by softness and beauty of the Borghese Gardens, and alive while exploring bustling neighborhoods pitched along the Tiber River. From the abundance of daily walking, my legs were sculpted and tan. I made my way back to campus every evening by sundown. Then I fit in with whoever wanted to drink.

• • •

On the twenty-first night of the trip, I found myself dancing on top of a wooden table. The nightclub resembled a gigantic cellar, pulsing with house music. It was deep underground, requiring taking an elevator that was positioned behind glass doors in a dark, narrow alleyway, and was guarded by two towering bouncers.

Earlier in the evening, the students had arranged a surprise toga party for the instructors to celebrate the coming of our final week. It was Thursday. When the party wound down at 8:00 p.m., a group of us scurried across town to the bars. I felt uneasy going out because we were scheduled to catch a train to Florence the next day at 7:30 a.m. But I went anyway. I didn't want to miss out.

The strap to my white, fabric, decorative backpack I'd bought from a street vendor broke while I was dancing on the table. When the backpack slipped from my shoulder, I gripped the broken strap in my hand, swayed my hips, and whipped the backpack—containing my passport, my school ID, and three hundred euros—around my head like a lasso. I released the strap, watching the backpack sail across the strobing rafters of the bar, over a sea of people, and out of sight.

Two hours later, blurry eyed, I crawled on my hands and knees along the filthy floor, between dancing legs, searching for it. By some grace of Roman, papal magic, I found it, blackened, under a bench, with all of my belongings intact. Despite the urgings of a classmate to wait for the rest of the group, I left the bar by myself. I tripped down the cobblestone alleyway clutching the torn bag in my hand.

Men in dark cars parked on the street jeered and shouted at me in Italian as I passed. I stretched my dress over my thighs. Headlights overlapped in a web of Bokeh. I reached out an arm to hail a taxi. A van pulled up, I climbed into the passenger seat, and handed the driver a scrap of paper from my wallet with the dormitory address written on it. We drove in silence. I was in a stupor. Halfway there, in scrappy English, he asked, "are you okay? Did someone hurt you?" I couldn't make words to answer the question.

At the dormitories, I ran to the bathroom and vomited. Then I stopped by the lounge area and bought a bottle of water from a vending machine. I wandered to my room and found my roommate, Brooke, who was also a social floater, passed out cold in her computer chair. She was sitting straight up. I shook her awake.

"How did you beat me home?" I asked. "I thought you were still at the club."

"No," she said, dazed. "I left by myself too."

We walked to the community kitchen to cook some food to soak up the alcohol in our stomachs. A third floater, Katie, who had also come home from the club alone, heard us from across the hall and popped her head in. The three of us opened the refrigerator and searched behind jugs of milk, vegetables, and blocks of cheese for our groceries to make a meal. Only, none of our groceries were there. Brooke peaked into the trashcan. There lay the discarded wrappers of our food.

Irritated, I left Brooke and Katie in the kitchen, walked back to my room, and returned with a notebook, tape, and permanent marker. I scrawled in huge, black letters on the notebook paper "WHO TOOK OUR FOOD?" Then I ripped the paper from the notebook and taped it to the fridge. The three of us stood quietly under the florescent kitchen bulbs with our arms crossed, hungry and dazed. The paper on the fridge, in all its boldness, looked a little ridiculous. Brooke picked up the note pad and marker and wrote, "I HOPE MY YOGURT WAS AS COLD AS YOUR HEART." We giggled and taped that note to the fridge too.

Galvanized, we passed the notepad around, writing more and more messages that we taped to the fridge, bulletin board, and kitchen walls. Pressure was building. The notes slowly exaggerated in intensity and profanity. The more absurd, the funnier they were. Combusting, tears streamed down our cheeks as we laughed doubled over and breathless. When we ran out of kitchen wall space, we buzzed up and down the corridors, kinetic, taping the notes to every bedroom door.

Students trickled in from late nights, pointing and laughing. They took pictures of the messages and flashed us thumbs up as they passed. Even the floor resident assistant came to see what the ruckus was. "Someone stole our food!" we protested. She rolled her eyes. "Just take everything down before you go to sleep," she yawned, and went back to bed. Our comedic genius enduring, we raided our art supplies to architect even more creative messages. Brooke disappeared, only to be found thirty minutes later in the men's restroom, having spelled "FUCK OFF" six feet tall on the wall, from electrical tape. The letters were so large they looked like a contemporary art installation.

By 6:00 a.m. we exhausted ourselves. One by one, we collapsed into our beds and fell dead asleep. At 7:00 a.m. my alarm went off. I snoozed it. I woke again at 7:15 a.m. to a fist slamming on the door. It burst open. A classmate stuck her head in. "What are you doing!" she shrieked. "Everyone is wondering where you all are. The train leaves in fifteen minutes!" I leapt from the bed, stupefied, threw open my armoire doors, tore a single dress from a hanger, threw it and a pair of flip flops into a gigantic suitcase, then my wallet, passport, and toothbrush.

The five items rattled around inside the empty suitcase as I dashed down the cobblestone street toward the subway. My dress, still unbuttoned down the back, hung off my shoulders as I shambled down the subway steps.

The train to Florence jerked along the rails and the blur of the scrolling landscape made me nauseous. A lock of greasy hair fell over my eyes as I squeezed my eyelids shut. Whispers fluttered throughout the cars. Students traded images snapped on cell phones and words like "terrorists" floated past my seat. Eyes darted over at me and my accomplices. We were seated in a row. "Don't worry," Katie yawned, still drunk. "Nothing's going to happen." I kept my face turned downward. My head was pounding.

At the hotel accommodations in Florence, the Dean summoned Brooke, Katie, and me to her room. She held the door warmly open for us. When she closed it after we entered, she turned coldly on her heel. "What *the fuck* did you do?" My mouth fell open. It did not seem like a possibility in my current reality the Dean of the art department—a polished, academic pillar—might ever use the word "fuck," no less in a sentence directed at me. But she did. And we were toast.

Discussions circulated all weekend between the Dean of UNF, the Dean of Saint John's, and the professors on whether or not to expel us. Not just from the Saint John's international campus that UNF had partnered with, but also from UNF entirely. As a starting point, Brooke, Katie, and I were instructed to write apology letters to our classmates, professors, and the Dean of Saint John's. We labored over these letters the whole weekend, pulling down the window shades to our shared hotel room, condemning ourselves only to the glow of a side table lamp. We took turns crying on the bed and pacing around the room. I cried so much that my eyes swelled shut. My stomach twisted and for three days I couldn't eat. Despondent, I mentally prepared to move back home to the wasteland of Ormond Beach. In a single night I had destroyed my future.

At the end of the weekend, we turned in our apology letters. At the Florence metro station, waiting on the platform for the express train to Rome, the Dean asked Brooke, Katie, and me to stand in front of the group who was seated on the ground. As she explained what we'd done and why everyone's curfew would now be set to 8:00 p.m., thirty hateful faces glowered at us.

Walking into Saint John's campus in Rome, the staff led us through the front door and directly into a dining room. Three chairs were pulled out at the far end of a long, dramatic table. At the other end of the table, the length of a shuffleboard court, peeking past ornate stalks of candelabra, sat the Director of Saint John's Campus Ministry with thirty-five crumpled sheets of paper in his hand. He read the messages aloud one by one. His voice and the wrinkling of the papers echoed off the hallowed walls. Because the notes were written in all-caps and black marker, he explained, the messages came across as hostile and dangerous. We were not expelled from UNF, but we were evacuated from the Saint John's premises effective immediately.

Security escorted us to our dorm rooms and monitored us as we quietly stuffed our belongings into our suitcases. "Do you have anything you need from the kitchen?" the guard asked. Brooke and I looked at each other, biting our tongues. We walked down the hall to the kitchen and the guard followed. We opened the refrigerator and stuck our heads inside, stacked over the other, like a Tiki. I heard Brooke start to giggle and I elbowed her in the rib. I slid open the bottom refrigerator drawer and two notebook papers stared up at us. "Where is my macaroni?" the top note read. "I will hunt you down," read the other. Brooke snatched them from the drawer, jamming them down the neck of her shirt into her bra.

Security walked us, with our luggage, to the sunny curb and locked the imposing, iron doors behind us. We took the subway to a residential area on the opposite side of the city and found an affordable, though cramped, hotel room, exclusively fit for a single person. Katie and Brooke waited outside with the luggage while I lied to the concierge that only I would be sleeping there and handed him a credit card my mom had given me for emergencies.

I went downstairs later that day and purchased a box of white wine from a corner store. I brought it to the roof and sipped it while the sun went down. My friends came up to join me.

"Do you want some?" I asked, gesturing to the wine box.

"No," Katie said, looking sick and surprised. "I'm not drinking for at least a month."

Brooke shook her head.

While my friends swore off drinking for the rest of the trip, I didn't see the point in it. We'd been spared and that was enough for me. A free radical, the sun glinted off my glass as I raised it to my lips.

8

PRESSURE

During the last semester of senior year, the design students were given appointments to come in and have their projects from over the course of the program reviewed. We were expected to choose the strongest eight to twelve projects and compose those into a professional portfolio by the end of the twelve weeks. We would use those portfolios to position us for jobs.

I went for my appointment and spread printed mockups of my projects across a row of desks, which included website wireframes, app designs, brochures, posters, wine labels, and so on. Pacing the desks, my professors looked worried. They struggled over which to choose. "There's barely enough quality here to even choose eight. You're going to have to redo everything. Use your time wisely."

In addition to full-time school at forty hours per week, I was working part-time as a waitress and also as an intern across town at the Jacksonville Museum of Contemporary Art.

When my roommates came home drunk on the weekends, slammed on my door, cajoling me to open it, I wouldn't. On my side of the door, I sat on the floor with papers scattered all over my legs, assembling dust jackets for a two-hundred-page book I had just finished hand stitching, or carefully maneuvering X-ACTO knife blades around die cuts in handmade CD sleeves.

Instead of drinking alcohol, a depressant, I started taking Adderall, a stimulant. My diet was the same every day: coffee, Red Bull, cigarettes, and a single chocolate chip muffin. All-nighters were common and, exasperated, I laid on the floor of my bedroom and pulled at my hair for hours. When I came to, sitting up at 5:00 a.m., split-end teepees littered my chest. My hair was becoming uneven on one side. I hid it by combing my bangs a certain way, or pulling my hair back in ponytails.

If my friends saw me pulling my hair, they smacked my hand away and said "Stop!" During my trips home, if my mom saw me pulling, she cupped her hand and held it beside her face to block me out of her vision. Shaming only made me pull more.

Neurologists have long been curious if trichotillomania—hair pulling—is related to OCD. Researchers conducted a study in 2017 using brain imaging to know for sure. The study was performed on seventy-six patients with trichotillomania and forty-one patients without. The brain imaging didn't show a relationship to OCD, but it did show similarities among Trich patients in the subcortical region of the brain: a "significantly increased thickness in a right frontal cluster." This is the region of the brain that suppresses motor response. The research indicates a malfunction in the mechanism the brain uses to tell us "stop, don't do that," in regard to a compulsive movement like hair pulling.[19]

---

19 Samuel R. Chamberlain, Michael Harries, Sarah A. Redden, et al, "Cortical Thickness Abnormalities in Trichotillomania: International Multi-Site Analysis," *Brain Imaging and Behavior* 12 (June 2017): 823–828.

One day, I showed Mom the penny-sized bald spots appearing around my head. Teary eyed, I pleaded "I don't know what's wrong with me, Mom. I think I need help. I can't stop doing it. I've tried."

These pleas were like distress signals. Flares firing in the night. But help never came.

"You just need to *stop*," she said. "It's a bad habit, like smoking. Just *stop doing it.*"

• • •

By the end of the semester I successfully assembled a professional portfolio of my work. I almost placed in the countrywide senior portfolio show. I was set to graduate in May 2013.

As graduation neared, pressure leaked from my sphere, and I let myself decompress. Home alone washing dishes one day, my phone rang. The caller ID read "Dad." Our intervals without speaking were extending. It'd been six months since we'd last spoken. I steadied myself and answered.

Lathering a soapy cup under the faucet, I positioned the phone on my shoulder.

"Hello?"

"Yeah, hey," he said, but his voice sounded different. Tight and strangled.

"What's up?"

"I just wanted to say I'm sorry. I'm sorry if I ever did things that hurt you."

He was crying. The words "I'm sorry," were new in his mouth and when the apology registered, my knees buckled. It knocked the wind out of me. The dish scrubber clattered into the sink. I lowered myself to the floor. The line was quiet. I pressed the phone to my ear.

"My dad was violent and that's how I remember a lot of our relationship. He was always shouting at me. I don't want you to remember me that way."

In a perfect world, I would have rewarded him for this. I would've said "Thank you for your vulnerability. I can tell it's difficult for you to say this. I really appreciate the effort and consideration it must've to make this phone call. It means a lot to me." But I didn't have those tools. Instead, I said nothing.

And then it was over. I blinked and it was gone. When he called again a few days later things were back to normal.

• • •

I had six tickets to my college graduation and none of them went to my father. I made this difficult decision for a few reasons.

Stress and drama, particularly during holidays, seemed to follow him. Growing up, while the holidays were meant to be celebratory, I braced myself for pain and conflict. Between bouts of feast and cheer, my parents fought over whose turn it was to see us and for how long, and if we were being picked up and dropped off too early or too late.

Once in high school, on Christmas day, I was helping my mom and aunt prepare dinner. I didn't have plans to see Dad, but I answered a phone call from him at 3:00 p.m. He announced he'd driven to Florida from Illinois and was staying with family three hours away. The RV had broken down and I'd have to drive to him. He asked me to do it that night. I was caught off guard and told him I needed a minute to think it over. When I called back, elbow deep in turkey grease, I explained I couldn't just up and leave. I asked why he hadn't told me he was coming earlier. He yelled into the phone "You're a selfish bitch!" and kept yelling until I hung up.

I had agonized for weeks on how I'd handle his attendance at graduation. *Who will I go to dinner with afterward, him or Mom? How will I take pictures with both of them after the event? What happens if a fight breaks out in public between them? What will I do? How will I control it?*

Weighing my options didn't feel good. It made me feel sick. Each option, to invite him or not, presented fear and loss, anxiety and confusion. All in all, I concluded the tickets should go to my mother, stepfather, grandparents, sister, and niece. I dreaded communicating my decision to him. So I didn't.

On the morning of my graduation day, Dad called me. I was lying in bed awake. The house was quiet. Sunlight filled the room. I assumed no one was home. I sat up and answered.

"Hi," I said.

"Hey there," he said, in a seemingly good mood. "Happy graduation day!"

"Thank you," I replied, relieved.

"Yeah," he said. "Now you get to go out in the world, find a job, and work the rest of your miserable life away." He released a raucous laugh. "So. What's the deal? Why didn't you invite me to it, huh?"

(Here it comes!) I cleared my throat. "Well. I just. I only had six tickets."

"Okay. *And?*"

My hands sweat. "I. I didn't have enough. You and Mary would had to have flown all the way down here and I didn't know how much time I'd even be able to spend with you. It just seemed like a lot to go through, coming all the way here and not knowing how to divide the time."

I could feel seething through the earpiece. "Oh. *Okay.* So you don't think as your *father* that I deserve to see my *daughter* on her graduation day?"

He was one thousand miles away, but it felt as though he were standing on my chest.

"No! No. It's just that I only had six tickets. And I needed to invite Mom, Steven, Grandma, Grandpa, Allie, and the baby."

"So why is it then that *Grandma* and *Grandpa* deserve to go and I *don't? Why is that?*"

I was floundering. "*I don't know!* I mean they gave me their car, which helped me get through college."

"Oh *okay.* So it's about *money!*" he yelled.

Now I was yelling. "*No.* It's not even *that.* It's just that, when you've come to events and things in the past, you tend to get angry, and upset, and I just couldn't deal with it today."

"*When* have I *ever* been upset? Huh? *When?*"

I was no longer in my bedroom. I was three years old, hiding from him in his apartment. "All the time! For *everything!* Are you seriously telling me that you could've been here today, around Mom's entire family, and not have started shit?"

"Wow! So *you* get to determine how *I* am going to behave *for me*? *Nice.* It's good that you've got a college diploma now to prove you're educated because you're a real *jackass.* A real fucking *dope.*"

While common knowledge might suggest I should've hung up the phone, history would argue differently. As my only frame of reference, I thought all parents spoke to their children in this manner. This was what we did. This was *normal.*

I was desperate to get the conversation where I wanted it to be on this very important day, supportive and loving, but trying to steer it back on course was like gunning a MAC truck over the edge of a jetty. The call escalated, as always, and I paced from room to room, hysterical. When I stomped into the kitchen, I stopped short. My roommate, who I shared a very thin wall with, stared back at me in his boxer shorts.

The writing was on the wall. Or rather on my roommate's face. His bewildered expression couldn't have been clearer. It read "*not normal.*"

9

PHYSICS

Like a glacier at first separating gently, and then in a deafening crack, roommates and friends disbanded. They moved back home with their parents, broke up, advanced serious commitments with their partners, or shipped off to graduate school.

I was burned out from my senior year. I decided to take six months off before finding a job that suited my degree. I waited tables at a breakfast restaurant and moved into a studio apartment alone. I was twenty-three years old.

The apartment I rented was on the ground floor of an old, fortified cement complex, shaped like a U around a dirty pool at the center. It was a block from the ocean. Wallpaper clung weakly to the interiors, damp from humidity, and forest green mildew spots blossomed from underneath.

Many assorted varieties of humans existed in this building, like the white man who hung through his kitchen window in the unit directly across from me. Each morning he pressed his forearms onto his window sill, leaned through the frame just enough to catch the sunshine on his forehead, and puffed on a cigar. He stayed there all day long. I made up stories about him in my mind. Like maybe he had tentacles for legs because I only ever saw him from the waist up.

I couldn't afford to both pay my rent and my student loans on my waitress's pay. Each month, I deducted money from my paltry savings to cover expenses. At the end of my six-month break, I applied for a job related to design that I found listed online. The title was Product Developer. It paid only slightly more than the breakfast restaurant, but it was something.

The company produced and sold collectible figurines. I was hired and placed in the "Ideation Department," pitching ideas in weekly meetings on what type of figurine I thought the company should produce next. Yorkshire terriers and fairies were best sellers.

I was assigned a cubicle. The particleboard dividers were arranged in a mazelike configuration, separated by a network of filing cabinets and shelving units, jam packed with papers, reports, and documentations the company had not yet figured out how to digitize. Figurines were stacked six feet high along the tops of the filing cabinets and on every shelf. From the bunker of my desk, I often wondered what would happen if there were ever a fire, surrounded by life-size tinder barrels of product reports and Dachshunds lacquered in flammable glazes.

Despite how often my parents discussed money and how important it seemed to have it, no one ever taught me what to do with it once it was mine. So I devised my own money management system, resembling something from the Great Depression. I deposited five hundred dollars into a digital savings account my mom had opened for me when I was a child. Other than that, I exclusively used cash. I divvied up the remaining dollar bills into paper envelopes labeled: electricity, rent, student loans, car payment, gas, groceries, and fun. The "fun" envelope stayed consistently vacant. I rolled a rubber band around the stack of envelopes and stashed them under some shirts in my dresser.

I enjoyed aspects of living on my own like cooking, walking around in my underwear, and leaving my belongings wherever I pleased. Every morning before work, I brewed a cup of coffee, walked down to the empty beach, and watched the sun rise over the ocean. I left my coffee cup in the sand and swam in the water with my clothes on. Broad tide pools reflected the sky, like mirroring sheets of otherworldly glass.

As special as these solitary moments were, without the distraction of roommates, the thumping of The Dread was loud and clear. I started going home with strangers I met at bars, allowing men to grope me in bar parking lots, or down in the inky blackness of the beach, desperate to echo what I'd felt with Aaron. One night, I happened upon a guy I'd known through mutual friends in high school. *At least he's vetted*, I thought. He got my phone number and we went on a few dates.

In the beginning of our relationship, he made me feel special. Like my attention really *mattered* to him. But I noticed some jealous tendencies that concerned me. At first, I wrote these off as idiosyncrasies, but his insecurities compounded. Highly suspicious, he began stopping by my apartment unannounced.

One night, I stepped out of my shower and answered a phone call from my mom. I walked around the living room chatting with her in a towel. I hung up the phone and was startled when, immediately after, I heard knocking. I peered through the peephole to see my suspicious boyfriend with his ear pressed against my door.

I removed the door chain and opened it.

"Who were you talking to?" he asked.

"My mom," I said, clutching the towel to my chest.

"Oh," he said, looking both relieved and disappointed.

"...What's up? Did you call me? I didn't know you were coming over."

"Oh. Yeah, no, I didn't. Just figured I'd stop by on my way home from work to see how you were." He lived *and* worked forty-five minutes across town.

"I'm good. Do you... want to come in?"

"No. I'm gonna go home and eat dinner."

My hair pulling fluctuated in ratio to his unannounced drop ins. After an especially terse phone conversation with him one evening, I laid on my bed, pulling, contemplating how to dump him. I stood up, walked to the bathroom, and turned my back to the vanity. I held up a hand mirror to see the back of my head. A quarter sized bald patch shown above the nape of my neck—the most I'd ever pulled in one sitting. My breath left me. I ran out of the bathroom, climbed into bed, curled on my side, and tucked my legs into my chest, taking the form of a shrimp. I picked up my phone and called my mom.

"What's wrong?" she asked sternly, hearing the tremble in my voice.

"I'm freaking *out,*" I wept, running my fingertips over the bald patch. "I have a quarter sized bald spot on the back of my head. I can't stop. It's never been this bad before. I think I need to see someone." My statements were more like questions, requesting a grant of permission.

"Okay," she said quietly. "Maybe you could see a psychiatrist. Or a psychologist? I don't think a regular doctor would treat this."

I sniffled.

"Let's try a therapist."

• • •

The day of my first therapy appointment, I pulled into a quiet, shady parking lot, and sat in my car with the engine running. I was early. My suspicious boyfriend called me.

"Hey," he said. "What are you doing?" I'd told him a few days beforehand that I was going to test out therapy. When he asked why, I told him "anxiety," which was true, but we both sensed there was something bigger, darker, circling under us.

"Hi," I answered. I noticed my voice sounded nervous. "I'm here. Just parked. Waiting to go in."

"Oh."

"Yep."

"Are you going to talk about *me*?"

I dug my fingernails into my palm. "I don't know. If she asks, I'm going to tell her I have a boyfriend." The digits on the car clock changed. "Okay, I have to go now, I don't want to be late. I'll call you after."

We hung up. His tone annoyed me. *Why is he so miserable?* I gathered my things. *How does my seeing a therapist have anything to do with* him*?*

The entryway opened into a quaint room with violet walls and some chairs. I took a seat. I honed in on a faint rhythm of voices beyond a door across from me. When it opened, a boy in an orange shirt stepped through, followed by a guardian, and then Anne. I stood to my feet and Anne smiled sweetly up at me. "You must be Nicki," she said. "Sorry I'm late. We ran over a few minutes."

We shuffled into her room and I took a seat on a sofa. *Huh,* I thought. *It really is like in the movies. I get the couch and she gets the armchair. Should I lay down?* There was a box of tissues beside me on a table. *I wonder if I'll cry,* I thought excitedly. I placed my purse on the floor and my phone faceup beside me on the couch cushion.

Anne was 5'3", white, eighty years old, with thinning rust colored hair to her waist. She wore a long, flowing, purple dress that matched her office walls and set her hair ablaze. Her presence was serene and a little mysterious. "So," she eased into the armchair, "we spoke a little on the phone, but can you tell me in more detail why you're here?"

It was notably quiet. I could hear blood pumping in my ears. "So I think I have a problem. I tend to pull at my hair when I'm nervous, well, er, sometimes I pull it *out* and sometimes I just pull at the *ends.* I looked it up and found some people online who do it too and I think it's called trichotillomania, although I know it can get bad, like *bad*, you know? Where people pull out whole heads of hair, or *eat* the hair, or *whatever*, but I'm not doing *that,* that would be *crazy,* I'm just pulling it out a little bit at a time."

A dial on a timer ticked across the room on her desk. I glanced at it. Beside it were heaps of papers, folders, and an ancient PC computer, preserved since 1970.

I took a breath. "I'm here because I pulled a quarter-sized patch of hair out of my head last week."

"Hm," Anne said.

My phone lit up from the couch and my eyes darted to it. So did Anne's. It was my suspicious boyfriend. I clicked the side button, rejecting the call. The screen went black.

"Okay," she said, "so I think I know a little bit about what's happening here, but I will have to look more into... what did you call it?"

My phone lit up again. I hastily clicked the side button. Then it lit up again, but this time a text message. It read, "Is your appointment over yet? Can I come over?" I grimaced and turned the phone over so the screen faced down.

"Who is that calling you?" Anne asked thoughtfully.

A bolt of something shot down my spine. "Uh. It's my boyfriend."

"Does he know you're here?" she asked, a genuine inquisitiveness.

"Yeah. He does. I just talked to him on the phone in the parking lot before I came in."

Anne examined her fingernails. "Hm. What does he want?"

"I think he wants to come over."

"Did you ask him to come over?" she asked, looking up at me.

I sat up a little straighter. "No," I said. "No, I didn't"

She raised her eyebrows into a question mark.

"Hm."

"What's your relationship like with him?"

"Um. Lately, it's been... weird."

"Weird how?"

I mulled over the events of last Saturday night. My suspicious boyfriend and I had driven to a pub in a neighboring town to grab dinner and drinks. At the end of the evening, he followed me into the women's restroom and cornered me in a toilet stall with my back to the wall. With one palm pressed into the wall over my shoulder he asked menacingly, "is my *penis* too *small* for you?" He wanted to know if that was the reason I'd stopped sleeping with him lately.

I ran out of the bathroom, out of the bar, and dove into some bushes like a maniac. I waited out there for thirty minutes until I realized I needed him for a ride home. On the hour long drive he suggested that I was a "whore" and, *tragically*, because of this, my vagina was too devastated to properly accommodate his manhood.

I didn't repeat this to Anne. I was embarrassed and ashamed, afraid of what she might think of me.

Instead, I said "He's been dropping by unannounced."

"Oh!" She stood from her seat, folded her arms behind her back, and paced the floor looking down. Her feet swished from under the robes. "And what else?" she asked.

"Um. He kind of scares me? He gets really angry sometimes. Not even necessarily at me, just in general. And mercurial. He exudes this energy when he's jealous that feels charged and scary. I don't know how to explain it, it's a brooding aura, like a black hole. My friends have stopped calling me to hang out. I think it's because he makes them uncomfortable."

Anne received this contemplatively. I didn't have to say anything else because the formula was recognizable. More than half of women who are abused as children go on to experience domestic abuse later in life. Domestic abuse in a child's home shows the child how relationships should be and what they should look like.[20] She didn't ask victim blaming questions like "Why do you stay then?" or "Why don't you just leave?" because Anne could see right through me—I was unconsciously reinforcing what I was taught I deserved. [21]

Her aura unexpectedly vivified. She returned to her chair. "Okay," she said, threading her fingers together. "He's got to go."

"Oh!"

"He's got to *go*," she repeated, boring into me. "These are the early signs of an abuser and you don't want to get in any deeper with him. I can tell you right now it will get physical."

Exiting her office at the end of our appointment, I tried to pay Anne with my cash, but Anne didn't accept cash or

---

20 "Crime and Justice: People Who Were Abused as Children Are More Likely to Be Abused as an Adult," Office for National Statistics, September 27, 2017.

21 Robert T. Muller, "Trauma Survivors at Risk for Future Abusive Relationships," *Psychology Today*, January 8, 2016.

cards. She produced a faded, yellow slip of paper from a stack of disheveled documents and scribbled out an invoice. "Just pay me for both sessions next time you see me. And next time bring a *check*."

• • •

Before my second appointment with Anne, I stopped by my bank that I didn't use, deposited some of my cash, and ordered some checks. This time, I placed my phone on her couch faceup.

She settled into her chair and glanced at it. "How is your boyfriend?" she asked.

"We broke up," I said, emotionless.

She looked pleased.

"I have been looking into hair pulling," she said. "We can try a few different things, but first I think we should try cognitive behavioral therapy." I didn't know what that meant.

She asked me to explain to her a little more about how and when I pulled and what physical and emotional environments I tended to be in when it happened. I told her. Then I asked "Can you maybe explain to me why you think I might be doing this?"

She smiled.

"Thousands of years ago our stress hormones served a more dramatic purpose. If we saw a tiger in the woods baring its teeth, our bloodstream flooded with cortisol and adrenaline, which caused us to react in a few different ways: fight, freeze, or flight. Nowadays, we don't have to remain on constant high alert for physical threats like tigers because we buy our food at grocery stores and sleep in houses. However, when we experience emotional instigations, our bodies might react to the perceived threat with the same intensity as if there were a tiger. Do you understand?"

I nodded.

"There are three parts to your brain," she continued. "The reptilian, limbic, and neocortex. The reptilian brain is connected to the brain stem. It's the oldest of the three and controls vital functions, such as heart rate, breathing, reflexive behaviors, muscle control, and body temperature.[22] It prompts us to duck if something is thrown at us, without us having to think about it.

The next part of the brain, the limbic brain, is the center of emotion and learning. It regulates feeding, reproduction, attachment behaviors, and evaluates events as either pleasurable or painful.[23] It doesn't register concepts of time or logic. Think of it like a security checkpoint scanning for threat or danger.[24] When the limbic brain signals danger, it activates the reptilian brain and the body automatically responds.

We've found in patients with post-traumatic stress that stress hormones continue to release for extended periods of time, alerting the brain of danger long after the threat has passed.[25] This is especially true for people who experienced their trauma in an environment where they were trapped.[26] The limbic brain has become frozen in the time when the trauma occurred.[27] If the trauma memory is triggered even by

---

22 Jamie Marich, "Reptilian Brain of Survival and Mammalian Brain," Gracepoint, accessed February 20, 2021.

23 Ibid.

24 Ibid.

25 Bessel Van Der Kolk, *The Body Keeps the Score: Brain, Mind, and Body in the Healing of Trauma* (New York: Penguin Books, 2015), 30.

26 Ibid.

27 Jamie Marich, "Reptilian Brain of Survival and Mammalian Brain," Gracepoint, accessed February 20, 2021.

something innocuous, no matter how much time has passed, it may incite the fight, freeze, or flight response.

When the reptilian brain is activated, the thinking brain shuts down. The entire left hemisphere of our brain that controls executive functioning, including our language center, deactivates.[28] It's impossible to process reason or logic when your body is shouting 'Run!'

If your mother was experiencing stress while she was pregnant with you, it's probable your brain was flooding with elevated stress levels in utero. Your reptilian brain is stuck on high alert with no resting state, always prepared for danger. And all of that energy needs expressing. When you pull out a hair or break off a split end, that's your body trying to release chronic anxiety. That's your body's way of soothing."

I stared at the wall, processing.

"Do you have any reason to suspect your mother was experiencing high stress when she was pregnant with you? How about in your childhood?"

Like apparitions, memories materialized. I described to Anne a vision I was having. "When I was three years old, I watched my dad rip a telephone out of the kitchen wall. He punched a hole straight through it. I remember he stormed into the garage after, yelling that he was going to get a sledgehammer. My sister jumped on his back and he wore her like a cape, as he waved the sledgehammer around in the air."

"That'll do it."

I sat in my car with my epiphanies after the appointment ended. My chronic anxiety was not my own, but a continuation of something inherited: either transmitted through my

---

28 Bessel Van Der Kolk, *The Body Keeps the Score: Brain, Mind, and Body in the Healing of Trauma* (New York: Penguin Books, 2015), 45.

mother and then to me, or sometimes a direct transference from my dad. I tilted my seat back and stared through my open window into the tree canopies. *How many generations has my anger inheritance passed through?* It seemed anger was like electricity, and people were like conductors. Anger circuited the power lines of my genealogy, neither created nor destroyed.

10

POSITIVE

I couldn't sit still. I bought a cheap bicycle from a friend and, every weekend, pedaled for eight hour stretches up and down the coast. I wore only a bikini, and some moccasins on my feet, which were ripping open at the fronts. My toes jutted between the stitching, barely holding the shoes together. No matter how often friends begged me to throw the hideous things away, I refused.

The moccasins suited my philosophy historically in accordance with my financial circumstances: "Ask for nothing" and "materialism is unnecessary." I could subsist as well as anyone else, wearing shoes my feet were bursting out of. These tattered moccasins were totems to prove it. I was all about getting by on the bare minimums.

And I did get by. I pedaled, and pedaled, and let myself become overwhelmed by the rush of wind on my forehead and the pummel of my heart against my chest. I carried with me only a water bottle, granola bar, and a book if I felt like stopping to read. I was very proud of this nakedness. The cyclical rhythms of my turning bicycle wheels generated an exoskeleton shedding. When I was on my bike, I was a woman molting.

• • •

Anne gave me some printed worksheets to fill out in between our visits. We also agreed I'd wear a rubber band on my wrist and snap it every time I felt the urge to pull my hair. Though, I didn't find this helpful. Snapping a rubber band against the tender part of my wrist didn't hinder me from wanting to pull my hair. It was just painful.

As our visits progressed, she asked more investigative questions about my life. "What do you do? Are you happy? What would you *like* to be doing?"

I explained I didn't feel like I belonged in Jacksonville Beach. My mind was ravenous for intellectual stimulation and culture our beach town was failing to deliver. I didn't have a graceful articulation of the totality of my depression, although it was really quite simple: I wanted *more*.

Elementarily, I said "I feel really stuck." I slouched on her couch. "I feel trapped here."

Anne smiled warmly. "Well, what do you think you'd have to do to become unstuck?"

I frowned. My couch slouch deepened. I was almost horizontal. I was liquefying before her eyes. "I don't have any money," I mumbled. "I guess I would have to apply for a new job wherever I want to move to. But isn't it rare that companies hire people who don't live locally?"

"Oh, no," Anne replied cheerfully. She wore glasses today and wiped the lenses on the hem of her flowery blouse. "It will happen very quickly. You'll be surprised. In the nearness of a month or two." She placed the glasses on her nose and they slanted over her wrinkled eyes. "Get ready. Once you start applying it's going to happen fast."

That was the last time I saw Anne. I was hired by an automotive marketing agency near Washington, DC two weeks later.

• • •

Moving has a strange way of making everything lackluster by its familiarity shine one last time. In the weeks before I moved, I ate at all of my favorite restaurants. I made appearances to say goodbye to my friends who remained. I even slept with an ex-boyfriend, a fun one, one last time. He drove me to my car in the morning, looking glum. As I transitioned from his passenger seat into my driver's seat, I felt an unwavering something inside of myself I'd never experienced after casual sex: *power*. Whereas I normally felt like something was being taken from me, this time I felt *emboldened*. The control felt so good I went out and did it again.

This time I texted a different ex-boyfriend—one who was never my actual boyfriend, but was on and off with me after Aaron for two whole years. A while back, when we were in the on stage, I flat out asked this OnOff ex-boyfriend to be my monogamous partner. He flat out said "No." I made it my challenge to change his mind, always using the offering of my body.

Once, while complaining about OnOff over lunch to a friend, my friend tried to give me some perspective. This friend was in nursing school and taking shifts in the hospice unit at the time. She said to me, "Nicki, I want you to close your eyes and imagine yourself at the end of your life. Imagine yourself as a very old woman looking up at your loved ones huddled all around you. Do you see OnOff there? Is OnOff at your side taking care of you?" My forehead puckered as I squeezed my eyes closed. No visualizations came. It wasn't that I didn't understand the question. I couldn't bridge the relevance of the question to the urgency of my desire, which was fueled by The Dread. I opened my eyes. All I saw was a Cobb salad.

The night before I moved to DC, I sat alone in my apartment on a futon, the only object not yet packed to be hauled across the country. My belongings were jammed into cardboard boxes towering all about, falling out of their containers. I pulled out my phone and sent OnOff the text. "Hey" it read. "I'm really sunburned and I need aloe. I'm soooo tired tho. Can you bring some over plzzz?" A champion of linguistic ciphers, he stopped by an hour later.

In the morning, as the sun crept over the lumps in my futon, the power feeling rekindled. OnOff even asked me to get breakfast with him, an especially rare invitation. I declined, which made me feel even more powerful. I walked him out and, in place of the distress that typically hijacked me after his departures, was *mightiness.*

• • •

I'd flown to DC two weeks before my employee start date to look for an apartment. I'd ended up renting the master bedroom of a five-bedroom group home. My job was thirteen miles outside of the city, so I nested near it in the suburbs.

When I arrived to the house to move in my things, the remaining four bedrooms had been filled by the landlord with men. Having already bonded, three of the new roommates were nice to me at least, and made me feel welcome. The fourth roommate, Ted, left me on edge. The night before my first day of work, he came home drunk at 3:00 a.m. after his bartending shift. He walked down the hall and hammered on my door. "Get up!" he shouted caustically through the wood. "Come have a drink!" I lay rigid and frightened beneath my sheets. The tips of his shoes cast shadows in the hallway glow that stretched across the carpet and under my door. Eventually he gave up, shouted "fucking lame!" and stomped down the hall.

The next morning, I drove to my new job where I'd be filling a role as a junior designer. The design team was welcoming, however, I observed the overall environment as feeling hierarchical. In a converted warehouse, an open floor plan, the project managers, who were all conventionally attractive and incomprehensibly polished, sat on one side of the room. The creative team, averagely attractive and awkward, sat together on the other. Each day the executives, an all-male cast, strutted into the building costumed in expensive suits and haircuts. Bleached teeth gleaming, they passed through the office kitchen and fist bumped sycophants who hovered near the coffee machine. Then they swaggered into their spacious, sunlit, private corner units. The rest of us proletariats hunched side by side over elongated tables arranged in rows, cramped on our side of the room.

I accepted all of the few invitations I received in my first week to attend lunches with my new coworkers. But some days I took my noontime breaks napping in the front seat of my car. I couldn't seem to stay awake throughout the day. I was uncharacteristically fatigued.

Mid October, the night was leaning deeper into daylight, darkening the sky by six o'clock. After work, I routinely went home, took a shower, and crawled into bed. I only had two friends in the area: Beth, who I knew from college, was engaged and occupied with her fiancé; and Brooke from Rome, who happened to live on the opposite side of the city, an hour's drive from my house. I was homesick.

I started a habit of interchangeably calling two of my best friends back home in Florida for nightly, after work check-ins: Abbie and Gabby. If one didn't answer I'd dial the other. I described to them what it was like in the suburbs of Virginia. They described what it was like in Florida. I was excited by fresh landscapes, metro systems, free museums, and a dramatic changing of seasons. I liked the almost abrasive vibrancy of transitioning leaves. I didn't yet miss the physical elements my old home offered as much as I missed the feeling of familiarity. Perhaps because we were tipping into winter, I sensed an inaudible constricting to the world around me. Like a preparing for something.

• • •

Eight days after I started my new job, a furious queasiness took hold of me on the drive home from work. I steered my hatchback into a gravel patch, fumbled with the plastic door-handle, and vomited into a ditch, hanging out of the open car door. I chalked it up to a sensitive stomach, but the queasiness reappeared the next evening. I sat in the work parking lot, tilted my seat into a reclining position, catching my breath.

The next morning while checking my emails at my desk, a sensation swept over me, an awareness I'd never encountered before. A *knowing.* I looked up and took inventory. My breasts felt sore. My body felt a little bloated. I couldn't recall the last time I'd received my period. I *knew.*

• • •

Back in college, a friend of a friend had stopped by my apartment in between classes to see if my roommate was home. My roommate was out, but I invited the friend of a friend inside anyway. She sat down at the kitchen table while I pulled a hot tray of steaming pizza rolls out of the oven. I asked her over my shoulder how she was doing.

"I'm okay," she said.

I shut the oven door with my foot and placed the tray on a loose oven mitt on the counter.

"Did Jackie tell you?" she asked apprehensively.

"No. Tell me what?" I replied, playing dumb.

"Oh." She stared at her hands on the table. "I had an abortion yesterday."

"Oh. I'm so sorry," I said, sullenly. "How do you feel?"

"It's okay. I'm okay."

The plastic spatula made a scraping noise as I shoveled the rolls one by one into a dish.

"This is my second one."

"Oh. Shit."

"I feel like a fucking idiot."

I set the spatula down. "You're not."

"Uh, yes. Yes, I am." She smirked and then started laughing.

I started laughing too. I brought the plate over to the table and sat down in a chair beside her. We quietly waited for the dough to cool. "Can I ask you something?"

"Sure."

"What does it feel like to be pregnant?"

She chewed the inside of her cheek. "To be honest, I just know. I don't know how to explain it. It's like your body wakes up or something. I've never carried a baby all the way to term, but both times I've just known."

• • •

I wanted to crawl out of my skin. I wanted to leave my body behind, sloughed off at my desk like a wrinkled flesh suit, to reappear in another life where I was not potentially pregnant or eight hundred miles away from anything familiar feeling.

But my body was *not* a removable skin suit. I *was* eight hundred miles from familiarity. I *was* potentially pregnant. And my lunch break wasn't for two more hours.

At noon, I stood up from my desk and power walked inconspicuously out of the building to my car. I had one hour before I needed to be back. I opened up my Maps app and drove twenty minutes to the closest pharmacy in complete silence. When I pulled into the parking lot my GPS directed me to, there was no CVS Pharmacy, only a small, dumpy grocery store. I circled the building twice, revolving like a predator, my hands trembling on the steering wheel. I cursed in whispers until I realized the CVS was inside the building.

I located the pharmacy in a dark corner of the store and placed a pregnancy test box on the counter. Summoning all of my fortitude to keep my expression emotionless, I asked the male pharmacist who was stuffing my dire purchase into a plastic bag "do you have a bathroom here?" He pointed to a shadowy corridor.

The bathroom floor and walls were outfitted with tile and every gesture I made created a deafening echo: the stall door squeaking open, the latch sliding into place, the rustling plastic bag, the swinging of my purse on the metal hook, the peeling of my tights down to my ankles. I revealed the slender test from the inside of the box and opened the superfluous instruction pamphlet. It unfolded like a road map of the continental United States and was typeset at a point size of five, the letters reading like scattered grains of pepper.

I had taken pregnancy tests before, but because of my intrinsic *knowing*, this time was different. There was absolutely no room for error. However, the directions may as well have been scripted in intergalactic dialects. I reread them three times before pulling the plastic cap from the fibrous stick and thrusting it between my legs.

I set a timer on my phone, and held the plastic wand in place. Finished, I placed the cap back over the fibers and set the test atop the dusty, plastic toilet paper dispenser beside me. Then I waited. When I picked the test up from its dirty perch, it was so lightweight it felt like a toy in my fingertips. *Surely,* I thought, *this tool established to deliver such* crucial *messages to its recipient should have more heft. Surely it should come equipped with infrared, heat-seeking capabilities, or bells, or a switchblade, or an emergency dial pad.*

As I peered into the plastic window the size of a water droplet that would bear my fate to me, it was not so far off an experience from the times I'd gazed into magic eight balls, desperately willing the alabaster prism swiveling below the murky depths to reward me with the answers I so wished to receive. And there it was. I squinted. A cross materialized below the glass.

A cross?

• • •

Everything encountered in this life is designed by a somebody. Even wild nature is shaped by the indirect implications man has on earth. So why then, I wondered, did the pregnancy test product designers settle on using a cross to represent "pregnant?" They could have used a circle, for example, representing the cycles of life. *Why the cross?*

A cross with equal length arms on all sides, like the one that rose to the surface of my pregnancy test, is known as the Greek Cross, the crux immissa quadrata, the square cross, the equal-armed cross, the balanced cross, the peaceful cross, and it's used by the Eastern Orthodox Church and in Early Christianity.[29]

The Pythagoreans, who embraced metempsychosis (the migration of the soul after death into a new body, human or animal) took vows on this cross. It was linked to their

---

29 "Info: Greek Cross," Greece.com, accessed January 23, 2021.

basic principle of the harmony of numbers and, by extension, *harmony of the universe.*[30] The equal armed cross has been interpreted as representing the four seasons, the four winds, and the four elements.

Due to its extensive and ancient use, the symbol is *loaded.*

Perhaps this is why it was seen fit to herald the divine effervescence of new life flourishing within me. Or maybe I read it wrong. Maybe it was just a plus sign.

• • •

The cross unhinged me from the anchors of gravity, and the world around me spiraled. I raised my sweating palms, planting them on the stall walls on either side of my head to hold myself up, but also to keep the walls from caving in. Under the weight of my collapse, my palms skated upward, across the surface of the walls, and my arms fully extended—my body taking the shape of the cross itself. My heart battered in my breast like a six-cylinder piston engine.

Once I steadied myself on the toilet, I felt a profound influence to mobilize. I yanked up my tights, stood up straight, rolled down my dress, snatched my purse from the hook, jammed the test back into the box with the crumpled instructions, thrust it into the plastic bag, tore out of the stall, down the hallway, past the pharmacy, past the pharmacist, through the electric doors dragging open for me as if by hallowed wizardry, through the parking lot, and into my car.

Speeding back to the office, I called Abbie. The world was still swiveling on its hinges like a Magic 8 ball prism, and I swerved across the road.

---

30 *Stanford Encyclopedia of Philosophy*, s.v. "Pythagoreanism," substantive revision July 31, 2019.

"Abbie," I gasped, "I think I'm having a panic attack."

"What? What's wrong?"

"I'm pregnant."

• • •

I completed the rest of my work day propped catatonically in front of my computer like a cardboard cutout. My mind raced over the nights I'd spent with my fun ex-boyfriend and then with OnOff. *How long ago was that? I thought we used protection? Whose baby am I carrying?*

It dawned on me that I'd found myself in identical circumstances to the people I'd seen on syndicated daytime television shows. Shows I jeered at, like Jerry Springer or Maury; shows I felt superiorly above. Shows where irate people clawed at one another over questions like "who's the daddy?"

Now I was the guest of my own syndicated daytime talk show. Except I was also the audience gaping at me in horror and humiliation. I was my own bouncer. I was the moderator. And there was no one to administer DNA tests.

I stopped at a gas station after work to purchase a pint of cookie dough ice cream. When I got home, I went straight to my room, locked the door, and ate the entire pint in bed. The ice cream tasted sweet and felt heavy inside of me, like it was tethering me to the ground.

When the weekend came, I spent it frantically applying for credit cards on my laptop in my bedroom, researching abortion clinics, and rifling through all of my on-boarding paperwork from my new job. I leafed through the printouts until I found some sheets detailing the health insurance coverage I'd opted for. I called the insurance company and they directed me to a PDF that stated what was included in my plan. Abortions were specifically excluded.

I tried calling all of the abortion clinics in my area to ask questions and set up an appointment to be seen. I left voicemail after voicemail. None of them were open during weekends. From my Google research, I gathered that to seek an abortion was to be served a terrible math problem. The cost of an abortion was dependent on the type of procedure, which was dependent on time. The sooner I was able to be seen, the cheaper it would be. It would take two more weeks for my first paycheck to process. Until then, I had the five hundred dollars in my savings account to last me for food and gas. The cost of an abortion pill in the state of Virginia was $455.

I had to wait until my noon lunch break on Monday to try again making calls to abortion clinics. This time I called from my car that I parked at a nearby strip mall for privacy. Again, I was received by answering machines. Abortion clinics were on their lunch breaks too.

I only told three people about my pregnancy: Abbie, Gabby, and Beth. I called Gabby crying that night and explained to her how my working hours were making it impossible for me to reach clinics. She promptly asked for my social security and driver's license number.

Tuesday morning, Gabby, who didn't have a day job at the time, called abortion clinics in my area, posing as me. During my lunch break, Gabby called me back. "I got in touch with Planned Parenthood. You have to have a phone interview with them before they'll schedule an abortion for you. I think it's an automated call, just listing information about the process. Your phone call is at 1:00 p.m. tomorrow. I gave them my, er, *your* phone number. They're going to call you."

I took my lunch break late on Wednesday, again from the strip mall parking lot. I had my automated informational phone appointment. When it was over, I spoke with a receptionist.

"Do you want to schedule a time to come in? We'll give you an ultrasound and then you'll come back for your appointment to take the pill. By Virginia law, we have to separate your ultrasound appointment and abortion appointment by twenty-four hours."

"Yes, please," I answered, relieved. I gave her my name, birthday, and anything else she asked for.

"The soonest appointment we have available is this Friday at 2:00 p.m. Can you do that?"

My stomach lurched. "No," I said woefully. "I literally just started a new job a week ago. I'm scared to ask for time off already. Do you have anything later?" I pleaded. "Like maybe after 5:00 p.m. so I can come after work?"

"Hm. I see an opening Friday at 5:30 p.m., but that's the absolute latest you could come in. We actually close at 5:30 p.m. Can you make that?"

"I'll find a way," I said.

Friday at 5:00 p.m., I bolted from my desk to my car. The clinic was exactly a thirty-minute drive from work in ideal, traffic-free conditions. However, I didn't know the DC Metro Area had scored that year as having the nation's worst traffic congestion.[31] At 5:15 p.m., I was trapped in a gridlock. I slammed my fists on my steering wheel and screamed so loud my throat burned. I cut across several highway lanes to exit, hoping to take back roads. The back roads were packed too. At 5:28 p.m. I was still fifteen miles away, barely moving. I pulled into the parking lot of a seafood restaurant and

---

31 Dick Uliano, "DC Tops List of Nation's Worst Traffic Gridlock," *WtopNews*, August 26, 2017.

desperately called the Planned Parenthood office. I didn't know what to say, maybe I would beg them to wait for me. The call went to voicemail. I dialed again. No answer.

11

SILVER

My sister gave birth to my niece when she was twenty years old. I was nineteen. My back was glued to the wall. Her contractions were quickening. I watched, alarmed, as Allie howled from a raised bed at the center of the delivery room on all fours like an animal. I'd never seen anything like it. Her face was red. "It hurts!" she screamed and whimpered. While childbirth was regarded in health class textbooks with an elegance harkening Claud Monet, this felt more like a Francis Bacon horror show. I waited (any minute now!) for her paper-thin bits to split open from the force of a head ramming through, gilded by low budget special effects. When she was crowning, I ran out of there. As far as I was concerned all mothers were champions of pain.

Sometimes pain really is love. Her baby emerged a beautiful, healthy, Renaissance cherub. Our family gathered in Allie's hospital room afterward, taking turns holding my niece. I was afraid. I didn't want to drop her. When it was my turn to accept her into my arms, I cradled her apprehensively in the crook of my elbow. Her head was warm and soft like a buttered dinner roll. The room dissolved. One by one we took in this new life. The infatuation in Allie's expression was matchless.

On the surface, no one knew what Allie was going through. She kept her personal matters separate from the family. A few months after my niece was born, my sister contacted my mother. She asked Mom to take my niece and raise her for a while because she was living in a dangerous environment and needed to get her own life straightened out. As she handed her baby over, she said through her tears, "I'm afraid I'm going to hurt her." I've always found this vulnerable admission on my sister's part, and her willingness to ask for help, evidence of her bravery, honesty, and strength.

• • •

By estimation, I was six weeks pregnant. It was glaring that I would not make it to Planned Parenthood based on their operating hours and location. I needed to find a clinic that was open on the weekends and closer to where I lived or worked. I searched online and chose the first clinic that came up in the search fitting this criterion. I made an appointment for the coming Saturday at 12:00 p.m.

In the meantime, my pregnancy inspired mixed emotions: terror coupled with fascination. At night, I stood in front of my floor length mirror and smoothed my open palms over my stomach. I studied how my breasts swelled, how my arms and thighs filled out a little more each day. My body was an answer to a primitive question that one can only truly know through lived experience. *This* was what it felt like to be pregnant.

When I first processed that I was pregnant, the first thought tethered to this information was, "I can't keep it." Though, I weighed my choices carefully. Some nights, I laid in bed with my eyes closed, imagining what this baby would look like if it came to fruition. *Would it have blue eyes or brown? What would its laugh sound like?* And during those visions, when I was able to produce them, I felt less alone. Like the baby in me was my truest companion. I wondered if I let this baby become my own, if I wouldn't have to be so by myself anymore.

Some nights I felt nothing at all. I was numb. From the movies I'd seen featuring abortions, the main characters were always visibly beleaguered with guilt and indecision. I held myself up against these references and interpreted my numbness as being "incorrect." To be the kind of woman seeking an abortion, to remain *good* and *moral*, I needed to feel contrition. So on the nights I felt nothing, I closed my eyes and tried even harder to picture my baby's face.

As human beings, we tend to compartmentalize the world around us into a dichotomy of *right* and *wrong*. This helps us digest the aggregation of our internal and external stimuli. But I felt helpless while compressed by this limited assumption. It has never been easy for me to attain such delineated clarity; things have always felt more abstract than black and white. My world is made of silver. Depending on where the light is catching, my perspective is ever changing.

However, in regard to my pregnancy, no matter how I rearranged the data, the factors, and the feelings, my intuition uncharacteristically led me to the same conclusion: no.

The purposes of soothing my own loneliness did not feel like a sound reason for me to carry a baby to term. Along with my visions of what the baby's physical traits would be, I also had visions of destitution and suffering. I needed to learn to save myself before I could save anyone else.

• • •

Whoever coined the expression "Money can't buy happiness," had surely never been single, regretfully knocked up, and broke.

I didn't know how I would pay for my abortion. I was chipping away at my five-hundred-dollar savings day by day. By Virginia law, I had six weeks to have a procedure before the cutoff date of twelve weeks. Additionally, I felt a mounting pressure in my moral code to halt the gestation as quickly as possible. I registered for my first credit card, but it might take weeks to be approved and mailed to me. I couldn't wait weeks. I'd need to ask for money.

When I first broke the news to Gabby over the phone, I asked her desperately, "I don't know what to do. Should I tell my mom?"

Gabby paused, considering this. And then she confirmed what I already knew "No. I really don't think that's a good idea. I think we can handle this ourselves." I asked my ex-boyfriends for money instead.

I sent them each a text message early in the day. At eight o'clock that night, I called them one after the other from the front seat of my dark car, which was turning into a personal office of sorts, parked in the driveway. I asked them both to pay for half the cost. They each sounded concerned, but for different reasons. My fun ex-boyfriend worried I would change my mind and decide to keep the pregnancy. I assured him I would not. OnOff worried he wouldn't be able to acquire a spare $250 to send me before his next scheduled paycheck in two weeks. He said he'd ask his boss at the coffee shop where he worked for an advance.

• • •

When I arrived to the clinic on Saturday, I was unsure if I was at the right place. I'd pulled off a high-traffic road into the parking lot of a stale, corporate office building. The parking lot was empty. I exited my car and walked to a glass entrance.

The doors were locked. Beside the doors was a doorbell, a speaker, and a camera pointed at me. Through the glass doors I saw an elevator lobby entirely shrouded in thin, clear, plastic tarps pinned all around the walls and floor, like a horror scene. I pushed the bell and a voice crackled over the speaker. It asked why I was there.

"I have an appointment at a women's clinic. Is it here?"

"Third floor," said the voice.

The doors vibrated when they buzzed, and I pulled them open.

On the third floor, I opened another glass door with the name of the clinic printed on the inside. The waiting room overwhelmed me. It was small. The size of my living room. Thirty women, some with children, were crammed inside. Plastic chairs lined the perimeter and made rows in the center. They were all filled with bodies. Some people were sitting on the floor with their backs against the walls. It was loud.

"Excuse me," a voice said sharply from my left.

I turned. A receptionist surveyed me from behind a desk. She wore black scrubs adorned by little purple and pink stars. Her eye was blackened and purple bruising, the same color as the stars, rounded the bridge of her nose and under her eyelid.

"Oh, sorry," I said. "I have an appointment at noon."

"Fill this out," she said, handing me a clipboard.

I walked past a pedestal elevating a glass dish overflowing with rainbow colored condoms wrapped in clear plastic, looking candied. I spotted a slim opening against a wall in a back corner so I walked to it and filled it with my body. I mindlessly filled out the multicolored forms, but it was hard to focus because of the noise from a film playing on several TVs positioned around the room, fastened to the ceiling. The volume was dialed all the way up and I recognized the film from the trailers. It was called *The Purge.* This is a dystopian horror movie where, for twelve consecutive hours, all crime in America—including murder—is legal.

I completed the forms and returned them to the desk. The receptionist accepted them, smiled, and said "we'll call you when we're ready." I went back to my corner and stood there.

After thirty minutes passed, I joined the others on the floor, sliding down the wall to a seated position. After an hour passed, a seat opened near me. I looked around. I moved to it. The crowd was thinning out slowly as patients were called back to see the doctor, but there were still many people before me. Two hours passed. Then three. *The Purge* had ended and restarted twice. It was playing on a loop. I couldn't bear to watch it, but I also couldn't not watch it because of how loudly it was playing. Blood curdling screams from the film reverberated around the room. The movie made me edgy and restless, but no one else was saying anything about it, so I didn't either.

After four hours passed, I was nearly the last one there. A nurse appeared at the front of the room. "Sorry, everyone," she announced. "That's it for today. We overbooked. The doctor is currently meeting with his last patient." She disappeared.

I looked around to meet the eyes of the remaining patrons in solidarity, but their eyes did not meet mine. When I walked to the desk to reschedule my appointment, the nurse who'd made the announcement seemed annoyed with me.

"Can you come Tuesday night? That's the soonest I can get you in. Tuesday evening at seven o'clock. It won't be busy like this. We'll be able to see you then."

• • •

I stopped at CVS on the way home to buy a pint of ice cream, which was an act I'd unintentionally turned into a nightly ritual. Each evening, I uncapped a tub of cookie dough ice cream, jammed a silver spoon into its mass, and levered it into my mouth while tucked under my bedsheets. I'd gained fifteen pounds in three weeks—more weight than I'd ever put on in a flux. The ovular contours of my figure were rounding. But eating ice cream at night invoked a unique and coveted sense of peace. My mind softened. All I was responsible for during my ice cream eats was: lift, swallow, repeat.

After dropping the ice cream tub into my plastic CVS hand basket, I turned the corner to the wine aisle and selected a bottle of Merlot. Even though my plan was to terminate my pregnancy, I hadn't felt comfortable drinking. I pretended not to know why on the surface because underneath lived a fear too scary to allow into my awareness, which was that my abortion would fall through. On top of that, I knew it didn't make sense, but, regardless, I felt a resistance to causing any incremental harm to whatever was inside me.

After four hours at the clinic, my depression overrode my ethics. I placed my items on the counter. The cashier asked for my driver's license. I fished it out of my wallet and handed it to him. He held the license up at eye level. He squinted at it and back at me.

"This isn't you," he proclaimed confidently.

I recoiled in shock. "...Yes it is," I said. My mouth was slightly agape.

He smirked. "No, it isn't." He handed the card to me over the counter. The tiny, laminated photo of my twenty-one-year-old face, smiling and jubilant, flashed on the card in the reflection of the overhead lights. Positioned behind the register was a TV screen streaming live feed from cameras positioned around the store. My black and white face was blown up on it in high definition. My appearance was haggard. My hair was scraggly and piled in a nest on top of my head. Darkened rings hung beneath my eyes. Everything was bloated.

I slid my debit card with my name printed on it across the countertop. "Look," I cried desperately. "It's *me*!"

He picked up the card and read it with his head sarcastically tilted. "But why don't you look like your picture?"

How much time do you have? Tears brimmed in my eyes, I snatched the card from his hand, jammed it into my purse, and left.

• • •

I drove to the clinic at seven o'clock on Tuesday night and was told they were closed. The receptionist who I'd last spoken to said she didn't remember me. "No one made an appointment for you." I went back the weekend after that, seven weeks pregnant, and was able to get an ultrasound. When I returned for my abortion, eight weeks pregnant, I was turned away again. The address on my Florida license didn't match my new address that I'd written down on the form, and they wouldn't let me change it. After each of these rejections, I sat in the parking lot with my forehead on the steering wheel of my car and wailed. Passing by the time sensitive weeks, while holding something I did not want inside of me, was agonizing. Arriving each weekend expecting the problem to be removed, only to go home still pregnant was devastating.

Having no control over what is occurring inside of one's body is torture. It is also the ultimate teacher. The loss of control humbled me. Some believe that we *can* alter the state of our bodies using our thoughts and, for the most part, I agree. Research has shown thoughts alone can improve vision, fitness, strength, immunity, and anxiety levels.[32] In my case, I was turned over to the forces of nature. I couldn't impede my pregnancy via the intensity of my thoughts. I was divided. The concept of my body separated from the concept of my consciousness that lives inside of it. My body was doing what it wanted. In all cases, involuntary developments in our bodies pose all the same questions: How are you going to *deal* with this? How are you going to *be*?

I don't know why it hadn't occurred to me earlier than it did to try to find a different clinic after my first poor experience. Perhaps because I'd already reached out to so many others, and my options were limited. Perhaps because I was not an abortion aficionado. Not much in the process came naturally to me. Perhaps I was experiencing pregnancy brain fog—confusion, forgetfulness, and fatigue. I was panicked and distressed. I felt extreme isolation from my friends, my family, and my job by my omissions.

At week nine, my engaged friend Beth checked in on me. I explained to her the dejected state I was in. She did an online search herself and found a different clinic open on the weekends not too far away. She sent me the phone number and encouraged me to go. I called and made an appointment for the following Saturday at 8:00 a.m. The receptionist confirmed I didn't have to come in for an initial ultrasound visit, since I'd already had one. I could come in to be treated as soon as possible.

However, I would be just beyond the legal time limit of ten weeks for taking the abortion pill. I would need to have a vacuum aspiration. The cost of a vacuum aspiration was

---

32 Ozgun Atasoy, "Your Thoughts Can Release Abilities Beyond Normal Limits," *Scientific American*, August 13, 2013.

approximately $500, plus an additional $100 for optional anesthesia. I opted in. "Call us when you're parked out back and we'll come out and collect you through a private door. Sometimes there are people outside with signs and they can be violent. We don't want you to experience that." The receptionist warned me I legally needed someone to drive me home because of the medication.

• • •

Three weeks had passed since my ex-boyfriends had sent me their shares of payment. That money was gone. I'd spent it on food, gas, and bills. I had $250 remaining in my emergency fund. My credit card hadn't come. I checked the mail for it every day.

Halloween passed. Thanksgiving was a week away. The Yule season was fast approaching. The last of fall leaves were perishing. The world was damp.

On Wednesday evening, three days before the $600 procedure, I had no clue how to pay for what was scheduled. I laid on the couch in the living room staring at the ceiling. It was dark outside. Someone had strung multicolor twinkle lights around the room and I let myself go cross-eyed in a self-induced hypnosis, gazing into a prismatic, motley blend of their glow. A screen door slammed shut. Someone entered the house through the kitchen. It was Ted. He passed through the living room and stopped when he noticed me sprawled on the couch. A rare sighting.

"Hey," he said, facing me from across the room.

I didn't look at him. Just continued crossing and uncrossing my eyes. My ankles overlapped, propped up on the couch arm. My hands relaxed in my lap. "Hey," I said.

He shifted his weight uncomfortably. "I'm about to have a beer. Do you want one?"

I knew the reason Ted was aggressive and rude with me was because he had a crush; like a child would do. But Ted was twenty-three years old and huge. His head hairs bristled the ceiling when he stood erect. Whenever I didn't respond to his antics, he reacted angrily to his feelings of rejection. This did not make me feel sorry for him, it disgusted me. Though, in the moment, I didn't have much else to lose. So I turned my head, pinned him in my gaze, and said "yep."

He spun around excitedly and trotted into the kitchen. I heard two caps clatter on the countertop, where they'd probably live forever, a far cry from a trash can. "Hey, you got some mail today," he chirped. I heard papers rustling and swung my feet to the ground, sitting up straight. He turned the corner, set the beer on the table, and tossed the letters beside it.

I picked them up and leafed through. Mostly a stack of direct mail ads, but underneath the lot was a personalized, red envelope with my name addressed in handwriting. The return address listed my stepmom's name. I slid my finger under the flap, tore it open, and revealed a Christmas card. *A bit early,* I thought. The text inside described how upset my dad was that I hadn't spoken to him in months. She asked that I please call him soon, to mollify his distress. Folded inside of the card was a $500 check.

12

RELIEF

On the morning of my abortion, the world was tinted blue. I left the house at 7:00 a.m. Few cars scattered the roadways. I blasted *Sleeping Lessons* by The Shins. My adrenaline increased.

The day had been carefully arranged. My procedure would take place at 8:00 a.m. Beth would pick me up at 10:00 a.m. and drive me home. I would spend the rest of the day asleep.

I pulled into the clinic parking lot and called the receptionist's desk as planned. Like she'd warned, people lined up on a sidewalk out front. They sipped from cups billowing steam, images of baby butchery hung slack at their sides. A nurse met me at a back door. I followed her through a tunnel that led to a bright, peaceful waiting room. Soft, ambient music filtered through unidentifiable speakers. There was an abundance of chairs, the majority empty, and sunlight streamed in through east-facing windows.

Upon receiving the check a few nights ago, while I should've been celebrating or crying tears of relief, again, I felt nothing. I was in shock. It seemed surreal that a flimsy slip of paper could dictate the next eighteen years of my life. I wasn't even sure how my stepmom had gotten my address, as I'd fought over the phone with my father the week before

I'd moved from Florida. When he'd texted, asking what my new address would be, I texted back "NO."

The check was so light in my fingertips, almost weightless, and yet heavy with expectation. I knew if I cashed it, my stepmom would see the money drain from her account. She'd expect a call from me shortly thereafter, a humble thank you. What was presented as a substantial early Christmas gift felt a lot like a bribe. If this were true, it positioned my self-respect and self-protection as something able to be bartered for.

The way I saw it I had three options: (1) Tear up the check, kneel at the nearest holy site, and pray for God Almighty to send my credit card before Saturday; (2) Save my ass and cash the check. Have an uncomfortable follow-up phone call, thanking my stepmom for the money. Or, the most radical and seductive option; (3) Cash the check. Interpret it as it was presented—a gift—and a *deserved* contribution to my wellness and future.

I filled out the paperwork the receptionist gave me and placed the clipboard on the counter. She checked her screen and said, "that'll be $600, please." Having already deposited the $500 check into my account, and transferred the last of my savings, she ran my debit card and the payment cleared. I breathed.

The nurses served me a pill and asked that I relax in the waiting room while it took effect. "In twenty minutes," they said, "you'll start to feel some cramping." This was true. I flipped through magazines, speculating what measures were occurring, why my muscles were contracting, while also not wanting to know. Forty minutes later, they took me to a private room and handed me a paper gown that tied in the back.

When I was changed, they led me to a larger, sterile room. A doctor orbited in the center on a swiveling stool, beaming like the sun. Beside him was a large metal table and an amalgam of tools, all whirring and beeping in consensus, a mechanical babbling. The air was ice cold. I shivered. He asked me to climb up on the table and lay on my back. Then to place my bare feet in the metal stirrups.

With every cautious step toward the table, flecks of me stripped away. Like on my long, Florida bike rides, I was molting. Except, this time, I was not losing myself, rather peeling down to my most fragile, delicate infancy. As sensitive and brittle as the sheet of caramel topping on a crème brûlée. As disarmed and scared as a brand-new baby.

"That's it, hop right up here," he cooed, patting the table with a latex hand. A nurse stepped forward, slipped her hand into mine, and helped me up.

A thin sheet of paper covered the table and it crinkled underneath my weight. Its texture felt like the realest, most human thing in the room. I laid back. The freezing metal shocked my naked back. My body trembled uncontrollably. The nurse holding my hand gave it a squeeze.

The doctor secured a clear, plastic mask over his face and then mine. Mine was oval, shaped around my mouth, and connected to a long tube.

"You'll be okay," he said, muffled. "Have you ever had laughing gas?"

I shook my head no.

He explained the technical effects. Then cracked a joke to make me laugh. The nurse smiled. "Alright, now I need you to count backward from ten when I give you a thumbs up. Can you do that?"

I nodded my head yes. The nurse squeezed my hand.

He held up his thumb.

Ten. Nine. Eight.

• • •

My consciousness yanked through a slit in the timeless, black void pit, and repopulated my gasping body. Someone pulled the plastic mask off of my face and my head lolled around on my neck, flaccid. As two arms threaded beneath my own, lifting me off the table and into a wheelchair, smears of my humanity, the hues of poppies, inside tangles of plastic tubes collaged, my periphery. Things not meant for me to see. The pair of arms glided me away from the whirring, beeping discord and into tranquility.

• • •

In the next room, they served me cookies and juice on a beige plastic tray resting across the handles of my wheelchair. The gas had left me happily serene. Several other women in paper gowns sat in wheelchairs beside me. We grinned at each other as we snacked on our treats. We drank our juice modestly together out of little paper cups, like well-mannered children. I liked this room. A nurse sat across from our row of wheelchairs, like our teacher, asking us follow-up questions. She pointed at pastel pamphlets with titles like "Gardasil" and "Birth Control."

Beth picked me up from the clinic right on time and we had a quiet ride home. She dropped me off in my driveway and when I entered my house everything was still. In line with my agenda, I removed only my pants and slithered into bed in the rest of my clothing. I lifted my phone to set an alarm. A text from OnOff appeared on screen. It read "All good?" I pulled the covers up to my chin and called him. I didn't want to seem needy so I made my voice happy and light, and reported I felt alright. But not that I also felt vulnerable and lonely.

"Get some rest," he said.

We hung up.

I didn't talk to my fun ex-boyfriend. A few weeks before my procedure he'd texted asking how things were going. When I tried to explain the upsetting circumstances of how difficult it was to be seen for an appointment, he went mute. A few days after that, he sent a curt text message that he was seeking work overseas.

13

REPETITION

My favorite moments shared with my mom are nested in the nothings.

Growing up, we did this thing. Late at night, when I was still small enough to fit into the kitchen cabinets during hide and seek, I routinely walked into Mom's bedroom wearing my white, *101 Dalmatians*, ankle length nightgown. The sleeves and hems of the nightgown were cuffed with pink frills that swished around my wrists and ankles. The fabric was worn and speckled with bitty balls of cotton pile. I found Mom lying face down on her unmade bed in her bra and unbuttoned jeans. The evening news played on the television propped above her armoire. The carpet in her room was bright pink. I moved my feet gently over it, until they carried me to her bedside.

I sat beside her on the mattress, which buoyed all sixty pounds of me. Her eyes were closed, but she sensed my presence. "Scratch my back?" she croaked into a pillow; a warm, but weary plea. The force of adult exhaustion perplexed me. I leaned over her and used the peach fingernails on my puny, girlish hand to scratch the broad, freckled skin that stretched over her back. "Lower," she directed, "under the buckle." My fingernails were new and soft, but they left vivid, red streaks easily on her skin. "Am I hurting you?" I squeaked.

"Wait! Right there. Scratch a little harder." My nails scratched and scratched. "Harder!" she cried dramatically, "really rip the skin!" We both laughed at the theatrics of this, not quite sure why it was so funny.

I only stopped scratching when she sighed, "*finally.*" I crawled under the blankets of the king size bed, bathing in a pool of side table lamp light, and watched the faces move on television. Without looking at her I asked her empty questions like "is there anything to eat in the fridge?" She answered incoherently from a dream. Eventually, she fell all the way asleep like that. I stayed in her bedroom for quite a while before climbing down from her bed and getting into my own. Each time, before I exited the room, she murmured "I love you," muffled into the sheets.

• • •

After the abortion, I lunged back into life. My job at the marketing agency wasn't paying me enough. So I got a new one. I downloaded dating apps, and decided I wanted a new boyfriend. So I got one. My roommate, Ted, was detained by police in the middle of the night for having a psychotic break. I decided I wanted a new place to live. So I looked on Craigslist and I got that too.

As quickly as these changes came, I didn't think too deeply about the nature of my newfound commitments. Like with moving away from home, I just wanted *different*—reacting to catalysts of *not this*. One of the trickiest parts of maneuvering emergencies is not necessarily juggling the emergencies themselves, but their robbery of preventative planning.

• • •

I laid in my new boyfriend, Jarred's, bed at ten o'clock on a Sunday night watching him fold laundry when my phone lit up. It read "mom." This surprised me. She was calling uncharacteristically late to break the news that she was experiencing a severe medical issue. Something potentially life-threatening. It needed to be managed quickly.

At the time, my relationship with my mom was complex. Even though I was over the threshold of adulthood at twenty-six years old, our communication was stunted. Not like with Dad, where things were openly and outwardly combative. With Mom, friction was woven into the passive aggressive unseen.

Over the years, our relationship had warped into a repetitious, looping series of mirroring and reacting to each other: both of us wanting closeness, but repelling each other at once.

While my mother was easily affectionate toward me in childhood, as I transitioned into my teens, I sensed her distancing. I needed emotional attention from my mom, but in the room across the hall, Allie was detonating. Feeling continually minimized, I grew equal parts resentful of her and desperate for her. This inward tension manifested in outward agitation. It showed in my mannerisms and the way I spoke, which alarmed and offended my mom. From her perspective, she gave everything. Extending into adulthood, the more guarded she became, the more overlooked and unimportant I felt. And the angrier this made me.

But then the 10:00 p.m. call came.

Circumstances that bring us toe to toe with death have a unique way of laser cutting straight through thickets of bullshit. Emergencies can invoke remarkable clarity.

When my mother started her treatments, I multiplied our usual monthly phone-calls to twice a week. I was petrified of what might happen to my mom. I mentally braced myself to fly to Florida at a moment's notice if things went south. Like with my abortion, because I'd never been in immediate proximity to a sick person, I unconsciously referenced what I'd absorbed through movies on how a person in my role should behave. I understood that sick people needed hope, and their healing depended on people who believed in them. What they needed were cheerleaders. During our phone calls, I clenched my abdomen and forced breezy positivity.

Her health crisis threw me into a deep depression. I felt my family was dissolving, drifting away in currents like splintered lumber in ship wreckage. I hadn't seen my father in six years. He was slowly unbecoming my father, progressively estranged. Though my sister contacted me every couple months with a new phone number, I felt she was lost too. The most I knew was that she was sharing a studio apartment somewhere in Florida with a man with rap sheets for selling methamphetamine. With the imaginable loss of my mother, I ruminated obsessively.

What will happen to me?

Friends and family reached out supportively when they heard the news. Though I welcomed the condolences, they were overridden by the loudness of my fear. The envisioned loss of both biological parents from my life consumed me: a primordial severing. All day long, day in, day out, at my desk, walking to the bus stop, eating lunch, riding my bike, checking my email, cooking dinner, doing laundry, watching TV, having sex, a concept repeated in my mind: *Orphan. Orphan. Orphan. Orphan.*

I considered returning to therapy.

• • •

In the spring, I planned for a June trip to Florida for Beth's wedding. I'd met Jarred through Beth, and he would be my date. I anticipated seeing my parents while in my home state, but I was nervous that meeting my family would be too heavy for Jarred. Because I was broke, Jarred offered to cover the cost of the rental car for the trip, which made me highly anxious that he get his *money's worth.* This included making it feel like a proper vacation for him. Packing, planning, and placating, I plastered on a smile and reassured him, "Don't worry! It will be *fun!* We'll go to the beach."

In June, the wedding went smoothly. Two days after the wedding, Jarred drove us in the rental car south to my parent's house where we would stay for a few days. When my mom and stepdad walked onto the lawn to greet us, I was happy to see them but my heart shattered. I'd never seen my mom in any state other than good physical health. The tells of her mortality that I'd never noticed before, threw me, threatening to sever us. My mother was supposed to be mine forever. Me to her and her to me.

Seeing her, I didn't know what to say. There is no literature that prepares us for the fragility of impregnated moments like these. Yet again, I found myself drowning in the mire of *right* and *wrong.* I didn't want to hurt Mom's feelings with an honest expression of how scared I was for us. Instead, I wanted to do and be whatever might restore her, which I'd already concluded was a cheerleader.

Jarred and I exited the car. I gave my parents each a hug. I smiled and made myself soft and calm. I hid myself in plain sight.

A critical question evaded me during this time of life, an inquisitiveness that might have helped us, which was to ask: *What do you need?* I didn't ask this question to my mom and I didn't ask it to myself. While I wasn't necessarily *wrong* by being a cheerleader, I missed an opportunity to connect more deeply with her by making assumptions. The dialogue might've changed from "Everything is going to be okay. You can do this!" to "Yea, this really sucks. I'm very scared too. But I love you. And I'm not going anywhere."

• • •

A month later, she called from Florida to tell me the doctors had scheduled a surgery that would involve a tool resembling a net. The surgery risks were severe, with a considerable variance dependent on microscopic tedium. Weeks passed and, as the surgery approached, my motor skills perceptibly slowed. I couldn't focus at work. I couldn't upkeep the energy required to placate Jarred. Eventually we broke up. Like there were perforations in my feet, the life source leaked out of me. Everything turned grey.

• • •

On the morning of the surgery, I called out of work. Then I called my mom. We talked briefly before she went into the hospital. I spent most of the day sleeping. Waking in spurts, I stared at the wall remembering an aquarium I had as a kid. I had begged my mom to buy me a beta fish to keep in it, and she obliged. The fish was beautiful, flashy, cerulean blue. Its name was Jerry. We placed Jerry in the aquarium on a shelf above the family computer. The first two weeks of Jerry's life, I fed him every day, appreciating his vibrancy through the glass.

As time progressed, my preoccupation with Jerry lessened. I forgot to sprinkle food pellets into his tank for several days.

Days turned into weeks. Jerry was visibly dead, hovering eerily in place. After a full month of neglect, my mom put her foot down. "That thing smells!" she shrieked, pinching her nose. "Take it outside." I wanted to give Jerry a proper disposal in our family toilet and the aquarium had come with a small, plastic net. I figured I should scoop Jerry out of the water with the net first, before dumping the dirty water from the tank into the yard.

I poked the mesh net into the water to gather Jerry up. When the tip of the net touched Jerry's body, he disintegrated into a billion smithereens. Dumbfounded, microscopic Jerry particles poured through gaps in the netting as it broke through the water's surface. He dissolved.

In the evening, I finally got up from my bed and drifted into the kitchen to make dinner. *Leftovers.* I pulled a Styrofoam box from the refrigerator and dumped a couple of cold crab cakes into a charred pan on the stove. It was dark in the house, but the oven light was on and I stood beneath the umbrella of its glow. I poured oil into the pan and it crackled in the rising heat. I considered the parallels between where my mother was now and my still recent abortion: both of us weathering undesirable removals; both of us riding the seesaw of life and death. One of the crab cakes was burning to the pan. I pulled a plastic spatula from a drawer and wedged it underneath. Smoke billowed from its underside. My phone lit up from on the counter.

I picked up the call and cradled the phone between my ear and shoulder, as both hands gripped the pan and spatula.

"Hey," my stepdad said, sounding hurried. Beeps and intercoms sounded in the background. I could hear pant legs swishing, as if he were walking very fast.

"Hi," I said, lifelessly. "How's it going?" I reached overhead and switched on the oven fan to clear the smoke. It roared.

"She just finished with the surgery. The procedure went well and they're wheeling her into the recovery room now."

I shoveled the spatula deeper beneath the crab cake and peeled it away from the pan. I swept it from the pan into a ceramic dish on the counter. "Your mother wants to talk to you," he said over sounds of more swishing. "She's pretty incoherent, but she insisted. Hang on."

I dropped my arm holding the spatula to my side. The oven fan buzzed statically.

"Hello? Nick?" Mom's voice was loud and clear, but sounded watery from the drugs. As if she were speaking from the depths of an aquarium, or the bottom of a dream.

"I'm here," I said nervously.

"I love you," she said.

"I love you too."

"I love you."

My stepdad came back on the line and we said our brief goodbyes, before he disappeared into a different world. I turned off the oven, left my crab cakes resting in the dish on the counter, walked out of the kitchen, into the dining room, and laid my eyes on a long, wooden bench pushed against the wall. I sat on it. Then I turned and laid down on my side and closed my eyes. I was still holding the spatula covered in grease. I unfurled my hand and let it fall to the wood floor. The house was smoky, but the fire was out.

PART THREE

14

BALANCE

Abbie and Gabby stopped speaking with me as much once the abortion was through. They were taxed from the outpouring of support I'd required, and it didn't need to be said with words. I respected this and let the space in.

I moved from Virginia into the city, on the north side of town, near Brooke. We hadn't kept up very much in the years since Italy, but both of us were open to new friendships. I reached out and we made plans to see a concert together.

I came by her house before the show to have a few drinks. Brooke lived with roommates too. She snatched some shot glasses from inside a kitchen cabinet, along with a bottle of whiskey, and led me upstairs. Sitting on her bed, we opened two bottled ciders from a six pack I brought with me, and dumped a shot of cinnamon whiskey into each of them.

"So," she asked brightly, "how have you been enjoying DC?"

"Um... It's been kind of crazy," I said.

"Oh, right, yeah. Because of the moving."

"Well… that and some other things. One of my old roommates, Ted, was admitted to a mental institution after running around the house with a butcher's knife in the middle of the night. He accused our other roommate of stealing money off of his dresser. The roommate called the police."

"Oh my God!" she exclaimed. "What did you do? Were you scared?"

"Nah. I slept through the whole thing, actually. I didn't even hear it." Brooke raised an eyebrow. I took a drink. "I was tired."

We listened to music and familiarized ourselves with the details of the past three years. After an hour or so, Brooke checked her watch. "Okay," she said "we *have* to leave after *this* drink!" Yet, like perennials blooming to life from death, full bottles of cider blossomed in our curled palms. One and a half hours later, we were each four loaded whiskey ciders deep. Brooke was laying on her back on the bed, and I was on my stomach on the floor. We were engrossed in a volley of hilarious and confessional truth telling.

"Yes!" Brooke cheered in conclusion to a secret she hadn't told anybody but me. "Can you believe that?"

"Do you know what *you* can't believe?" I asked from the carpet.

"What?" She peeked over the edge of the mattress at me. Her hair was tousled and her eyeliner was smeared. The warmth of my cheeks beamed red at her like a toaster oven.

"When I moved here, I was pregnant. And now... I'm *not*."

"*What?* With who? Or *whose?*"

"*Who's to say?*"

Dead drunk, we rolled around her room cackling like the beer bottles rattling in her plastic trash can. We missed the concert but discovered something exceptional in each other.

• • •

While all of my other relationships had much movement to them, Brooke and I created a special bond just by sitting in place. I drove to her house after work every Friday night, picking up wine and a pizza on the way. We ate the pizza and drank the wine while applying our makeup and doing our hair, preparing to go out for the evening. Most times we never made it out the door.

Truthfully, those nights when we didn't leave were my favorite. For hours, anchored to the bed, we laughed until our makeup dripped off. We watched videos on her phone, gossiped about ex-boyfriends, and made stupid faces at each other. We discussed our lives, our families, where we wanted to go, and where we'd been..

The more time we spent together, The Dread within me eased. Sometimes we pissed each other off, but I innately understood Brooke, and she understood me. Nobody had to prove anything.

Some nights we had sleepovers, which felt childish, but sweet. In the mornings, we propped ourselves u against her headboard, listened to podcasts, and sipped coffee. We camped together so often, when loading up my car with bags, and chairs, and utensils, bottles, and baubles, we were so synchronized we rarely had to speak. We read tarot cards by candle light, mythologized our futures, and ate psychedelic mushrooms on Assateague beach.

Yet, having long sought this type of closeness, trust, and familiarity, I forgot even good things need to be measured. No seeable signpost marked "too far" where our separate selves enmeshed. It was steadily harder to distinguish if what was best for Brooke was also best for me, and vice versa.

• • •

Three years had passed since my visits with Jane. Right before I broke up with Jarrod, I sought out another therapist. The pressure of my mother's illness had been too much to bear on my own, but I continued seeing my therapist even after Mom's successful procedure. We met during my lunch breaks every two weeks. Her name was Ramona.

Ramona was taller than me at 5'9", Black, and in her late thirties or early forties. Her long hair was twisted into box braids, sometimes interwoven with silver threads that glistened in the overhead office lights. Our incremental visits were like following bread crumbs toward a big, blurry goal. I wasn't sure exactly what I was working toward. I simply wanted her to help me feel better. I needed her to tell me what to do.

A month into our visits she asked me, "how do you shower?"

"What?"

"Like, do you just get in and out? Or do you take your time?"

"I don't know," I said, thoughtfully. "I don't really think about showering while I'm doing it. I just do my routine and then hop out. I'm usually in my head."

"Okay," she said. "I want you to try something. Next time you take a shower, when you're in there, I want you to try closing your eyes and focusing on one sensation at a time. Pay attention to how the warm water feels on your skin. Focus on how the steam helps open up your sinuses while you're breathing."

I went home in the evening and did what she said. I put my phone down, where I thought my life was, turned on the warm shower water, and sat down on the bottom of the tub. I closed my eyes and slid the bar of soap around my legs and focused on its drip running down my shins. I focused on the sensations of the water beads striking my chest and the sound of its spray against the shower curtain.

The antidote to hypervigilance and depersonalization is presence.

While hypervigilance does require a heightened sense of presence, what I experienced in the shower was different. Hypervigilance caused me to live inside my mind, rapidly and unconsciously synthesizing patterns. My overactive intuition protected me from danger by consistently drafting predictions.

Depersonalization did the opposite. It required me to abandon myself, to go numb by dissociating when I experienced pain or need. It kept me from eating when I was hungry, from resting when I was tired, from leaving uncomfortable circumstances. My dials were haywire, too sensitive and too numb all at once. Simple tasks in the shower, like closing my eyes and feeling the soap lather my belly, showed me what equilibrium felt like. I thought less and I felt more.

From then on, with every shower, I practiced slowing my mind and remaining in my body. This is how my Ramona tricked me into meditating. This is how I came to know attention as a large part of love.

In these stages, I was lightyears from perfect. But the goal wasn't big and fast, the goal was small and slow. The next small and slow thing we focused on was creating a routine. Though I took my basic life-sustaining systems for granted, like breathing, eating, sleeping, and digestion, these systems create internal balance known as homeostasis. When one of these systems is off, it throws off the body's entire equilibrium.[33] To standardize my systems, we started by adding small bullet points on my schedule every month, like "eat

---

33 Bessel Van Der Kolk, *The Body Keeps the Score: Brain, Mind, and Body in the Healing of Trauma* (New York: Penguin Books, 2015), 56.

breakfast before leaving the house" and "drink a cup of tea before going to sleep."

With childish innocence, I was recreating myself. These small, repetitive tweaks made me like a beach dune, changing shape imperceptibly in real time. Though, if I looked away for a while and looked back, my contours were perceivably shifting.

• • •

Since my phase of extraordinary ice cream consumption, my body had changed and stayed that way. I'd gained twenty pounds. The weight in and of itself didn't bother me tremendously, but what the weight represented haunted me. I felt uncomfortable seeing myself. I was carrying my baggage, literally.

I've always had an affinity for cardio over weightlifting because I like what movement does for me. So I started running. Running required minimal materials and was free. All I needed to depend on was me. I ran during my lunch breaks or after work. I ran around public parks on the weekends, and up and down the steps of the Lincoln Memorial in the mornings.

Initially, I aimed for a weight that felt natural to my frame, but running became less of a means to an end than it did a form of expression. To quote ultramarathon runner Ann Trason, I found running *romantic*. "What could be more sensual... than paying exquisite attention to your own body?"[34]

Forever, I'd treated my body like a pair of shredded moccasins that my toes burst through. I wore it down to the fringes, starved it, parched it, exhausted it, drank it to death, and abused it sexually. My new commitment to running,

34 Christopher McDougall, *Born to Run: A Hidden Tribe, Superathletes, and the Greatest Race the World Has Never Seen* (New York: Vintage, 2011) 55.

unbeknownst to me, was not only to a sport, but an undercover initiation to *knowing* myself.

The demand of its sensations kept me localized inside my body. I curated playlists for my runs with specific beats per minute, which helped me drop my footsteps into sync. I drank water and ate healthier food that provided me with more energy. I examined my aches and pains. I tracked the frequency of my heartbeats. I slept deeper. I measured the pacing of my breathing. I felt happier, lighter, and more relaxed afterward. I stretched and foam rolled muscles individually. Running helped me identify my body not only as a tool, but as a home.

I found I felt most alive while running on trails. I delighted in leaping over root tangles, darting around switchbacks, and dashing between boulders with mud caking my sneakers. I enjoyed the softness of the landings after leaping and the forgivingness of soil over concrete. It brought back the enchantment of my childhood, tromping through underbrush, sidestepping rattlesnakes, dodging poison ivy, poison oak, stinging nettles, wild boars, leeches, snakes, deer ticks, regular ticks, turkeys, and turkey vultures.

Whether it was camping, hiking, and now running, I felt most myself while in nature. Whoever I needed to be while I was in it was *correct.* I kept an Eckhart Tolle quote close to my heart, "When we go into a forest that has not been interfered with by man, our thinking mind will see only disorder and chaos all around us. It won't even be able to differentiate between life (good) and death (bad) anymore since everywhere new life grows out of rotting and decaying matter. Only if we are still enough inside and the noise of thinking subsides can we become aware that there is a hidden harmony here, a sacredness, a higher order in which everything has its perfect place and could not be other than what it is and the way it is."[35]

Nature made me feel this way inside of my own life. Nothing inside or outside of me needed to be managed or rearranged. In the woods, I just *was*. Nature was the only place I felt perfect as I am.

My frame was getting fitter and leaner. The ice cream weight had long disappeared, but I wanted to keep going. I signed up for 5K's, then 10K's, and eventually readied for a half marathon. I never knew I could run so far, and I wanted my first half to be special. In November, I Google searched "half marathons trail running." I discovered a small, unpopular race occurring a few months down the road in February 2017, listed at Montara Mountain, just south of San Francisco in California.

I told Brooke about the race while eating pizza in her bed on Friday night.

"Don't do it," she said, biting into her crust and shaking her head. "It's not a good idea."

"Why?" I asked, with my mouth full of cheese.

"Because you're broke," she stated, practically. "And you'll have even more credit card debt than you do now. Trust me, traveling is expensive."

I chewed my pizza. I didn't argue a case for myself because she was right. I was broke. Nor had I ever traveled that far away by myself before. I had no idea what I was doing.

I trusted Brooke. I had reverence for her guidance. She knew me better than anyone. She wasn't afraid to tell me difficult truths.

---

35 Eckhart Tolle, *A New Earth: Awakening to Your Life's Purpose* (New York: Viking Press, 2005) 194–195.

But the shower had taught me something new. There was something about the race I couldn't let go of. Later in the weekend, I sat in the tub, turned on the water, and listened. Like searching my fingertips along the ledge for the loofah, I felt around inside of my heart.

From my desk at work on Monday morning, I booked my spot in the half marathon. Then a round-trip plane ticket to California for February.

15

AUTONOMY

I rented a bed in a hostel in San Francisco for the first week of my fourteen-day trip. The hostel was on a grassy hill near the wharf. My bed was one of thirty in the room—I slept on the bottom bunk—which smelled wholly of feet. I rented a locker in the lobby, but the lock pad felt like a toy, so I kept my shoes, makeup, and toothbrush in it, but slept with my wallet and car keys under my pillow.

At first, I was timid to be so alone and so far from the east coast. Unlike the Rome study abroad program, which my mom had largely arranged for me, and where I was part of a group, California was all me. I felt awkward and unhuman doing even ordinary things, like figuring out how to get food and where I should eat it. For forty-eight hours, I was out of place everywhere. And then, an overnight phenomenon, I found my bearings.

My anonymity liberated me and I became strikingly *free*. I immediately belonged everywhere. I visited art museums, parks, beaches, gardens, and landmarks. I wandered curiously into an erotic shop all by my grown-up self for the first time in my life. I prowled Valencia Street at night, drinking beers and watching live music underneath a disco ball. I flirted with a cute bartender and was invited on a laughably expensive yacht by a laughably old man. I drove over the Golden Gate Bridge to Muir woods, ambling through sheets of mist blanketing midriffs of redwood trees.

When filled with intellectual, visual, physical subjects I loved, non-belonging transformed into autonomy. I felt electrified, emitting unseeable magnetism to the vicinity. Strangers initiated uncharacteristic conversations with me in bars or in the streets. Clearing the hold of habitual life revealed elements of myself I didn't realize I possessed. Motivated *toward* pleasure and curiosity rather than *from* fear and pain made all the difference.

• • •

The half marathon was scheduled on the seventh day of my trip. I departed the hostel before sunrise and headed toward Montara Mountain, which was an hour drive. I was charmed by the starry winks of buildings staggering up the San Francisco hillsides.

I pulled into the parking lot at the base of the mountain just as the race was beginning and the sun was rising. As I stepped out of the car, I heard the whistle sound. I zipped my car key into the pocket of my leggings and jogged to the starting line. The start was empty, which meant the group had already taken off. I jogged through the entry flags and just kept going. Hustling, I was already out of breath by the time I caught the tail end of the group. The trail was narrow—one foot wide and steadily rising. The group was snaking upward, single file, and packed together tightly. There was no room to pass. I caught my breath and settled into last place for the time being.

A mile in, the trail leveled out and widened. As people relaxed into their pacing, distance between runners expanded, and I gently shouldered my way forward. It had rained the night before, so the trail was slopped in mud. I *relished* this. It lent the race aesthetics an element of savagery. The trail whipped us downhill, uphill, and downhill again, like a roller coaster—ruthless but riveting. I kept balance with impressive control as my sneakers skidded over the steepness of slick stones and muck. The terrain alternated between soaking jungle and craggy, mountainous bluffs as it changed elevation. Inhales swelled my lungs with perfumes of damp, morning eucalyptus trees.

Ascending the mountain along endless switchbacks, we headed for the peak at two thousand feet. I yanked my windbreaker knotted at my waist and covered myself with it. The high-altitude winds tore at my cheeks. The higher I rose on the gravel path, the panorama dilated, encompassing breathtaking vastness of the ocean. Grinding forward, I sucked in freezing breaths of salty air.

I knew I was getting close to the peak when the front runners whipped past me on their way back down. Finally, I crested. Situated at the very top was a looming radio tower. At the base of the radio tower was a crate filled with colorful wristbands. Racers were to wear these to prove they had completed the course. I darted to the box with the other runners dashing up the hill behind me. We grinned hugely at each other in our sprints, the way lunatics who share secrets do, embellished by gorgeous, arduous scrambles. I snatched one from the bin and rolled it over my wrist, a little rubber trophy.

The descent from the peak was nearly straight down. I'd learned in my training not to lock my legs on descents or resist gravity. The advice I'd gotten was "just let yourself fall." However, for thirty uninterrupted minutes, I didn't just fall, I flew. I soared over clay coated boulders, and around crooked, dusty bends. I plunged into shadowy eucalyptus tunnels and surged into the sunlight. I hailed the agility and nimbleness of my feet.

At the bottom of the mountain, up ahead, I spotted a station with tables and snacks. *The finish line.*

"Whew!" I belted, exasperated, as I trotted up to the table. A short, white woman, with cotton fluffed hair handed me a paper cup.

"There's Coke in there!" she piped.

I gulped the liquid down and crushed the cup in my fist. "Where's the other runners?" I asked, beaming. It was deserted.

She looked confused. "They're running."

"But the ones who've finished, where are they?"

"Finished? This is only halfway. You have seven miles left!"

The second half of the race routed us back up to the peak, down again, and across a valley. My muscles were screaming, but I savored these sensations. Between the flush of scenery, blasting the Rolling Stones in my earphones, and endocannabinoids flooding my brain, trail running was euphoric. Not just during this race, though especially during this race, but always. With all five senses maxed out, there is truth in that I loved running so much because it mimicked the intense highs that alcohol and sex could bring, wild from the inside out. Though, instead of breaking down my brain, or alienating me, running built me up. It improved my mood, executive functions, and memory.[36] Driving forward in a flock of other runners, I felt a sense of camaraderie. Running in the wilderness was a covenant to *living.*

• • •

---

36 Malissa Rodenburg, "From Memory to Motor Skills, Running Improves Brain Function," Women's Running, July 2, 2020.

After crossing the *real* finish line, I stood in line for a bowl of homemade chili at the small afterparty. A man in line in front of me turned and started a conversation. He was tall, tan, and attractive, with bright blue eyes.

He asked how I did. "Great!" I said. "I finished in seventh place in my age group. How did you do?"

"Second," he said. I waited for a qualifying category, but then I realized he meant second place in the entire race. "I think I could have gotten a better time, but I tripped and fell." He showed me a sludge smear decorating his entire leg. "I also got lost at one point." We both laughed and I told him I did too, which was true. We chatted about how the mud had been tricky and he flashed me the bottoms of his sneakers. They had little screws he'd twisted into them for traction.

"Do you run other races with this group?" he asked

"No," I said. "This is my first half marathon, actually. I knew I wanted to do a trail run, and I happened upon this race online. It looked really cool. So I flew here from Washington, DC."

"Oh!" he said, looking surprised, and then impressed. "This is a really good one for your first time. I'm not from here either, originally. I'm from the East Coast, Gainesville, Florida."

"Whoa!" I exclaimed, "Me too! I'm from Ormond Beach."

We collected our chili bowls and sat down at a picnic table across from each other. "I really like it here so far," I said, slurping the hot beans. "There's something really compelling about the landscape. Everything is so robust: the cliffsides, the waves, the mountains."

"Yea," he answered, popping open a soda can. "Once I moved here from Florida, I knew this was it for me." He took a sip of his drink and leaned in over the table. Baby blues glittering, he whispered, "this place has some kind of magic."

When we finished eating, I walked alone past the parking lot, down to a grassy knoll overlooking the ocean and laid on my back. I listened to the waves crash into the shoreline and remembered reading Henry Miller's descriptions of Coastal California in college. He'd described the sea-beast-rock-boulders as the elbows of the sea, but they looked more like beautiful goiters to me, right in the throat of the ocean, bellowing a guttural opera.

Clouds resembling buffalo deities grazed overhead in a broad field of sky. The drive of the waves shattering on the sand was so powerful it rattled my sternum. I felt at home here, in all the drama of the topography. It suited me. I rolled onto my front, peeking meekly over the edge of the precipice, so as not to disturb the natural elements playing like a chamber ensemble below.

If I'd consulted the figures represented in my checking account before the trip, on whether or not I should've flown across the country for a fourteen-day vacation, they would have resounded in a collective "hell no." Though I knew I'd made the right decision. Muscles easing in the grass, everything in my body cooed an undoubted "hell yes." Some experiences exist in and of themselves, but others may reap benefits extending far beyond the parameters of time within which they occur. Some experiences, although costly in the moment, change us for the rest of our lives.

• • •

The morning after the race, I couldn't raise my right leg. Trying to lift it felt like all the times I tried to bend spoons with my mind using telekinesis as a child. The results were the same: nothing happened. From aggressively skidding on the trail mud, I'd pulled my hip flexor. Nonetheless, I managed to check out of the hostel, prepared to spend the second half of my trip in Yosemite National Park. I threaded my fingers together underneath my thigh, lifted it up, and swung my leg forward into the driver's seat of the rental car. I was ready.

February is the rainy season in California, which I did not know until I got there. The overcast drive to the National Park was still remarkable. I rose to elevations I'd never been. I stopped on the shoulder of the road to take pictures of alien-looking fauna, growing only at such dramatic heights. However, when I arrived in Yosemite it was late, 5:00 p.m. As I passed through the entrance booths, it started pouring. A ranger poked his head through a small window and explained that my primitive campsite at Camp 4 was self check-in. And also, it had been raining there for four days straight. So the site was flooded. "Good luck," he said, and handed me a receipt.

I wound around the dirt roads searching for my campground past sprawling fields and creeks that opened onto gargantuan rock walls the size of God. I folded over the steering wheel and smooshed my face against the windshield to take it all in. Stoic only for a moment, I exploded into unexpected weeping at the surreal bigness of this gift I'd given myself. Gratitude rushed into my chest.

• • •

The ranger was right. Camp 4 was soaked. Few campers remained and, luckily, I found a patch of earth slightly tilted so the water drained around it. Still, I noticed it pooled in places, as the ground seemed to be made of tightly packed dirt. The sun was going down and I needed to set up quickly while I could see. I laid out a tarp and tried pinning it down with stakes. The earth was too dense for the stakes to go in, like concrete. I looked around for boulders and rolled them over to my site, pinning the tarp down with these instead. I continued erecting my eight-year-old tent, bedecked with ribbons of duct tape that patched holes near the entry, but the tent had never let me down before. *Good enough.*

I rushed to the park store to buy some groceries and a butane tank for a small, cheap camp stove I'd purchased on Amazon. I was happy to have brought it, as the wood in the area was drenched—slim chance of building a fire. All I brought for a light source was my phone, a small flashlight, and a couple of weak glow-sticks. I banked on purchasing some candles too.

By the time I got to the store, it was closing in fifteen minutes. I paced the aisles grabbing anything edible and tossing it in my basket: eggs, apples, a pack of six mini wine bottles, canned beans, cheese, tortillas. A voice sounded over the speaker, "Final purchases please. Five minutes until registers close." I sprinted to the utility aisle, searching for candles. There were none.

I ran to the front of the store and asked a clerk urgently "Hidoyouhavecandlesplease?"

"Oh, hmm. I don't think so."

My face dropped.

"Actually, I *do* think we sell birthday candles. Would that work?"

"Yea, sure, whatever." I shrugged in a panic.

He pointed and I snatched the birthday candles from a rack.

Think, Nicki, think! How to make light?

"Last call for shoppers," said the intercom voice.

Okay, I thought. *Yes. This is what I'll do. I'll makeshift some sort of candle holder of my own. Isn't that all a lantern is anyway? Just a candle carrier? I just need to fill a cup with something dense and jam some candles in it. Okay. Right.*

I flashed across the store, grabbed a small jar of applesauce, and set my basket on the cashier's counter just as the overhead lights flipped off.

When I got back to Camp 4, it was pitch black. The rain was relentless. Streams of water the size of small creeks rushed between tent sites. Fortunately, my sleeping bag, along with a duffle bag, were already in the tent. I only had to make two more trips carrying over my suitcase and the groceries. I tossed my things into the black innards of the tent, just as dark inside as it was outside. I realized I needed light to see better. Then I could start cooking and have something to eat. I hadn't eaten since I'd left San Francisco eight hours earlier. I was light-headed and my hands were shaky.

I pulled the birthday candles and apple sauce from the grocery bag and wandered beyond the perimeter of the tarp into the dark. I hated apple sauce. I dumped it out of the jar into a trash bag, and planned to fill the empty jar with dirt. As I kneeled to the ground and scraped it with my fingertips, scratching wet soil into sad, mushy piles, I recalled that the dirt wasn't actual dirt. It was some stiff, weird ingredients, too dense to pitch a tent stake through. The rain hammering the back of my head, cloaked by my jacket hood, was deafening. I tilted the empty jar and swept whatever I could into it with my hand. I lifted the jar to eye level and what mud I'd scooped into it sloshed around inside looking just as soggy as applesauce. Woozy, I scraped at the ground even more desperately than before.

Just then, a star exploded over me. I was blinded by a detonation of the sun. I squinted over my shoulder and the silhouettes of two, exotic aliens curled over me.

"What are you doing?" one of them hollered over the rain.

The beam of a headlamp strapped to its forehead emanated like the powerful augury of a third eye. I squinted into the light, raindrops striking my open eyes. I barely made out the faces of two, handsome blonde men. Their accent was Scandinavian. Not aliens, but beauties.

I glanced down at my hands. In the light, my fingernails were blackened, covered in mud, and I realized how feral I appeared—alone in the dark, fingering freezing sludge into an applesauce jar. The temperature was at most thirty degrees. My knuckles seared red across the backs of my hands like garlands of cherry tomatoes. The birthday candles lay strewn in the dirt.

A burst of panicked breath released in a mist, captured by the headlamp light ray. "Uh. I just. I thought maybe, like... I don't know." I searched for a reason, stammering. And then just, "Honestly, I don't know."

"Okay!" the beauty said cheerfully. "Well, we have a fire going nearby if you'd like to join. We have drinks, food, and room for another."

I followed the beam of his pointed flashlight to a luxurious, blazing fire at the center of their camp, kept dry via an overhanging tarp.

"Okay," I said. "I think I'll just um... finish up here. And... maybe!"

"Alright," he said. The beauties looked at each other and continued walking. "Stop by if you feel like!"

I stuffed the jar and wet candles into my pocket and crept to my tent where I planned to die privately from embarrassment. I unzipped the door, crawled inside, where the inky darkness was everything. I pulled a birthday candle from the plastic package in my pocket and lit it with a match. It was then, not in the store, that I remembered how quickly birthday candles burned. Its flame eliminated in eight seconds flat, into a petite puddle of wax.

I sat back on my duffle bag, vexed. Then felt wetness. Reaching behind me, my fingers touched water. I rummaged in the duffle, pulled out the small flashlight, and clicked it on to find water pooling on the floor. My sleeping bag was wet. My equipment was wet. I accepted defeat.

Besides the Scandinavian beauties, everyone in Camp 4 had gone to sleep. I was disappointed that I wouldn't have the experience in my tent I'd anticipated, but the rental car offered warmth and dryness. Switching gears, I decided to relocate everything to the car and sleep in the backseat. The rain lightened a bit as I dragged my suitcase out of the tent and onto the tarp. I shoved the car key into my front jean pocket, then clicked the small flashlight on, and positioned it into my open mouth, facing out. I bit down hard on the plastic handle with my front teeth: an improvised head lamp. I picked up my suitcase and carried it in my curled forearms toward the car, stepping over water streams gushing between pine needle piles. I was almost home free when a voice called out to me. I froze.

"Excuse me!" the voice cheered.

With the flashlight in mouth, my head swiveled slowly on my neck looking like a lighthouse.

A blonde woman, snuggled in an expensive looking coat, called to me from a bulletin board at the edge of the parking lot.

"Do you know anything about how to check in?"

I was genuinely stunned to be spoken to under the circumstances. Instinctively, I released the tension in my jaw to reply. The flashlight slipped backward and I made a choking noise, remembering I had a plastic torch lodged in my throat.

She ogled me, eagerly awaiting.

Can she see me? I asked myself, glaring at her angrily. *The audacity!*

My arms were buckling under the weight of the suitcase. I bent my knees, going low to gather a better grip, and the suitcase slipped off my wet forearms. It jabbed me in my already weakened hip and pressed through my pocket into the car key. The car alarm activated, which released ear splitting sirens that carried across the park.

I flinched at the sound and the suitcase fell to the ground. The zipper burst open, my clothes exploded from the inside, and dumped into the streaming mud. I stared incredulously at my feet. Tents rustled. I fumbled for the key in my pocket, pressing a red button frantically, which quieted the car. I looked around for the blonde woman. She was gone.

Making my car into an apartment, I draped my damp clothing over the backs of car seats, over the rearview mirror, and along the dashboard. I spread out my sleeping bag in the back seat and turned up the heat. I strung shirts over the windows for privacy and hung glow-sticks from handles in the ceiling.

I was relieved my sleeping situation was taken care of, but I was starving. I gathered the camp stove and butane, and stood beside the car in the dark, sliding the connective pieces together. Though I couldn't get them to latch. I hiked over to the women's restroom to use the overhead light fixed over the exterior porch. Beneath the floodlight, I stood against the wall and fiddled with the devices. Even when I connected them, I could hear gas hissing out, but the flame wouldn't catch.

Two women from the Scandinavian campsite smiled at me as they walked into the bathroom. Their hairs were twisted into braids like golden pretzels. I smiled back politely, then glowered at the device sizzling in my hands. I flicked the dial on the stove once. Then again. The third time I heard a pop. It burst into a flaming ellipse. I dropped it and the gas, spraying from one end like a tail, rocketed the stove around the porch, spinning it 360 degrees

OHMYGODOHMYGODOHMYGOD.

I looked wildly around the deck, made entirely of wood, and considered the women inside. Fear jolted through me. *I'm gonna burn this mother to the ground!* The women emerged from the bathroom. They took in the scene and looked at me, shocked, all our mouths hanging open. "Snow!" one shouted and pointed to a patch of it. We scooped it up with our hands and dumped it on the fireball whizzing around the deck. When the blast was out, we folded over on the ground in fits of laughter.

Back at the car, I tore open a mini wine bottle and gulped the entire thing. Then I gulped another. I peeled off my wet clothes and opened the cold can of refried beans. With the enormous can positioned in my naked lap, I tore the disks of a tortilla into bits, dunked them into the bean can, and folded them into my mouth. They tasted marvelous.

When my mono temperature feast was complete, and I'd downed all six mini bottles of wine, I bagged up the trash and readied the back seat for sleep. I positioned my down winter jacket against the car door for a pillow. I switched off the overhead light and the glow sticks swung overhead like a psychic's pendulum, writing incantations over me. From the outside, the car looked like a radioactive cocoon or something out of a Marvel magazine.

My final errand, I grabbed the flashlight and walked the trash bag a quarter mile to some metal trash boxes down the road, in case of bears. Pleasantly drunk, I swung the bag lightly at my side, flashlight beam dancing on the path ahead. Then, out of absolute darkness, a phone started ringing. Not a cellphone, but an antiquated jingling. I halted in place, heart pounding. Rotating cautiously to my left, the flashlight washed over a row of blue, old fashioned pay phones. I couldn't believe it.

Not only was it strange to see a payphone in any regard in 2017, an apparatus of the past, it was extra surprising to see one at the top of a Sierra Nevada mountain, on a deserted road, at four thousand feet, in the blackness of 1:00 a.m., ringing.

If a payphone rings in the forest in the middle of the night, and there's no drunk woman passing by to throw away her wine bottles, does it even make a sound?

Who would be calling here now? I anxiously begged the air. *Is someone waiting for a call?* I stupidly swept the flashlight across the darkness, but I was alone. There were no Western specters of John Wayne hanging around, arms folded, patiently awaiting a long-distance buzz. Each ring was a maddening responsibility. *Who was on the other end? What would they say to me?* I debated if I should answer, but my terror locked me in place, outweighing curiosity. The whole thing felt utterly ridiculous. Staged, even! And yet... a ghostly, antediluvian payphone was undeniably ringing. The universe was calling me.

• • •

At 7:00 a.m., the sun filtered through the T-shirts covering the windows. I laid on my side, wedged deep inside my sleeping bag like a lima bean. A seat belt thrust into my vertebrae. I shrugged the sleeping bag down to my naked shoulders and peeked out the back window of the car. The campground was empty. I wasn't surprised. It was still raining.

By the time I pulled on a shirt and clambered into the parking lot to stretch my legs, a sign was tacked to the Camp 4 bulletin board. It read, "Campground closing at 4 p.m. due to incoming storm." I opted to at least go on a day hike before I had to leave. I pulled on my down coat, laced up my hiking boots, and embarked on a climb to Yosemite Falls.

My hip flexor had considerably healed overnight, so I could better lift my leg today. Still, I took my time pausing to examine lichen and various mushrooms. I passed a gargantuan log with a hole in the center. The wood had splintered open in a sensational orange splatter, its colors saturated with a deluge of rainwater. I lodged my entire head inside, upside down, sucking in clouds of fresh pine.

In Muir woods, the week before, I'd learned the term nurse log: a fallen tree that provides its surroundings "ecological facilitation" as it decays, offering seedlings shade, nutrients, water and protection from disease and pathogens, thus nurturing and making way for the new generation.[37] Romanticizing the nurse log's efficiency and altruism on its demise, with my head upside down inside of it, I cried sweetly.

Three miles in, I came upon a waterfall and squeezed myself into a small cavern made by the rocks behind its spray. The rocks curving overhead sheltered me from the rain. My knee-length down coat was like a sponge and had soaked up so much rainwater it was more water than down, weighing, I imagined, a cool six hundred pounds. However, the rain absorption made it dense, like a wall. Though it should've made me colder, it trapped in all my body heat. I kept it on.

One of my socks was drenched too. Water and snow had leaked in through a hole in my boot sole—a site where the rubber had burned through from placing my feet too close to a fire pit in Shenandoah with Brooke last fall.

---

37 Allie Wisniewski, "Nurse Logs: Healers of the Forest," *American Forests* (blog), *The Official Blog of American Forests*, July 12, 2017.

Behind the waterfall, I relaxed and removed my backpack. I pulled out a pen and small pad of paper. I rested against the boulder and jotted down a memory that fluttered into my mind. I remembered sitting with Allie against a brick wall in childhood after an all-day field trip to Universal Studios. It had rained that entire day too. Allie was crying while waiting for our mom to pick us up because her feet were unbearably waterlogged. When she removed her shoes the soles of her feet were easily mistakable for the faces of two small Chinese Shar Peis. Like a miniature Brigadier General, I'd ordered her, "put your shoes back on and suck it up."

I closed my eyes and reflected on our relationship. I'd always kept journals and diaries to log thoughts and feelings over the years, but I'd been writing a lot more lately, even starting a small blog. I sometimes found the transcriptions of my memories were more like questions rather than answers.

Mist from the waterfall stippled my paper and the sheet wilted. I closed my notebook and stuffed it and the pen back in my bag.

Toward the end of the trail, the wind was fierce, and the rain turned into snow. I walked just far enough to gaze upon impressive Yosemite Falls, one of the tallest waterfalls in North America, then turned around to head back.

At the car, everything was again damp. I opened all four doors and stripped off my down coat, rain jacket beneath that, sweater beneath that, boots, socks, long johns, and the jeans over those. Behind the car wheel I blasted the heat. It was 4:00 p.m. The campground was closed, and I had nowhere to go. Homeless, I stared through the windshield wearing only my cotton underwear and a long-sleeve T-shirt. I plugged San Francisco into my phone GPS. I turned the key in the ignition and simply started driving.

Since Yosemite National park is a U-shaped valley that was formed thousands of years ago through glacial erosion, the roads leading out of it escalate to dizzying heights at six, seven, then eight thousand feet. I looped around turns in a daze, and the sun emerged from behind the clouds for the first time all day. From an aerial perspective, I gazed down below at the impressive rock formations sculpted by incremental weathering. The sun cast a golden halo across the Sierra Nevada mountain range that rippled into the distance like pairs of gnarled hands. I rolled my window down and my mouth fell open at its profound artistry. "ETA 10:52 p.m." chirped the GPS. I was nervous at my aimlessness, but not scared. I had glimpsed what I was capable of. Each passing moment was merely a footfall forward in the sequence of my becoming.

16

RELATIVITY

By the time I flew back to DC from California, Brooke had landed a job across the country. When she told me in March that she would be moving, I was happy and excited for her. Although, she was my primary support system and I was hers, so the separation was stressful on both of us. We got into an argument and fell out in the week before she left.

After a rigorous four-month interview process that had started back in October, I too had landed a new job at National Geographic, but I would be staying in DC. The transition felt unsteady and difficult, while at the same time promising because my outer purposes were aligning more with my inner values.

My romantic life followed suit. I had been dipping in and out of flings for a year, but in June things became more serious with someone. We'd connected for the first time right after my breakup with Jarred. His name was Eric. I met him in the street.

• • •

Twelve months earlier, shortly after my mom's procedure, I was pressured into attending my roommate's birthday party at a bar across the street from our house.

"Come *on*," she said, stomping a foot. "It's my birthday! There will be cute guys from my job there." She winked.

It was Friday evening after work. I slumped in a wooden chair at the dining room table at 7:00 p.m., my pajamas sagging around me. "I don't need any more guys," I declared, scrolling on my phone.

"Okay, then just come for me! For an hour. Please?"

I looked at the ceiling and sighed. "Fine. For an hour!" I schlepped into my room and wrestled a rumpled white and pink tennis dress from my hamper. I hadn't done laundry in weeks.

The bar was in a basement. I didn't know anyone at the party except for my roommate who was busy hosting. I idled near a pillar and sipped my drink. In my resting gaze, I noticed a tall man with a sharp nose and curly hair step in from the street. My mom always teased me that tall, curly-haired men were my thing and, setting eyes on him, my stomach flipped. He shuffled to the bar between people on stools to order a beer. I looked away.

When I turned my head back in his direction, he was walking straight toward me. I stopped breathing.

"Hey," he said, directly at me.

I was stunned. *Oh my god.* I thought. *I'm a witch!* "Hi." I answered apprehensively.

"You cut me off."

"What?" My face flushed. Warmth crept over my chest and up my neck.

"You cut me off," he repeated. "Two weeks ago. Down in Noma on K street. You were riding your bike west and I was in the bike lane riding north. I had the right of way, but you rode straight through the intersection without stopping. You even looked right at me when you did it." I was stunned. I stared at him, unblinking. His posture slackened a little and he sipped his beer casually. He moved in closer and gazed out at the room, as if we were paired.

"Are you *sure* it was me?" I asked.

"Yea," he asserted. I could smell the cologne on his neck. He laughed and licked the foam from his upper lip. Then nodded at my dress. "Your bike has blue wheels and you were wearing that, actually. That's why I recognize you."

"Oh!"

"I thought you were cute."

We spent the rest of the party talking only to each other, then closed the night out dancing at a club next door. I invited him home with me.

While forward in public, our dynamic was different in private in the weeks following this encounter. He was quiet and reserved. So Zen that his supreme calmness made me clumsy and overly aware of myself. Silence between us made me anxious, and I tired myself out with empty prattling to fill it. Our only commonalities seemed to be a mutual adoration of Labrador Retrievers, and our jobs related to climate science. I was skeptical, but he was attractive, intelligent, and ambitious. When he confessed he didn't want a girlfriend because he was moving soon for graduate school, *bingo,* this drew me to him unfailingly.

• • •

For a year, Eric and I entertained a long-distance repertoire of chasing and running. Rhyming with my dating history, he visited DC every two months, slept with me, then disappeared. Though sometimes he did unpredictably romantic things, like driving seven hours through the night to surprise me on my birthday. If ever I started a relationship with anyone else, he showed up unannounced on my doorstep to fight for me. He wanted me, but he wouldn't have me all the way.

Then something changed.

Eric visited DC in June of 2017, right before flying overseas for a two-month research project. He texted me on a Sunday afternoon and asked if he could come over. When I opened the door, he looked stressed. I let him inside and led him upstairs to my room. He sat on one end of my bed and I sat on the other. "I want to do this for real," he announced. While he expected this to flatter me, his certainty was highly unusual and made me uneasy. *What's the catch? Does he just want to reserve me for himself until he gets back to the states?*

"How about this?" I countered. "It doesn't make sense for us to start something right before you leave the country for two months. Why don't we use this opportunity to practice communicating consistently? Let's start by sending each other emails every week. If that goes well, we can re-evaluate things when you're back." He agreed.

According to our deal, if Eric's email appeared in my inbox on a Friday, I was to wait a whole week to reply, and vice versa. At first, communicating this way was awkward, as physical intimacy was our fluency, but the more we emailed, the more I found his writing unexpectedly titillating. His internal voice was observant, even poetic, but not saccharine. As a fail-safe, I continued to flirt with people at parties and give out my phone number, but I eagerly anticipated Eric's emails. I checked my inbox every day, and when one appeared, I opened it immediately.

The architecture of our communication over email heightened wistfulness and longing. I was an eighteenth-century war wife penning letters to her groom. As the two months drew to a close, the frequency of our emails accelerated from once a week to every day. Mid-August, a week before Eric was scheduled to fly back to America, his last email read, "I just called the airline. I changed my return flight from Connecticut to Washington, DC. See you in seven days."

• • •

The theory of the multiverse is reliant on another theory called "cosmic inflation," originated by physicist Alan Guth. Cosmic inflation describes a possibility that offshoots of our single universe can occur, generating ever-increasing numbers of universes.[38] Scientists coined the expression "*multi*verse" because they found that what they had called the "*uni*verse" could be divided into extremely large regions, which may have different laws of physics.[39]

I imagine that time is not fluid throughout the multiverse, but elastic. Like a cartoon flip book, time speeds up, slows down, even pauses or retrocedes. Ten hours may feel like two minutes. Two minutes may feel like ten days.

Life as I'd known it for twenty-seven years had existed only in one, singular universe. However chaotic, the passage of time was at least linear. On the day Eric revisited me, a quantum tunnel ripped a hole through the wall of reality.

3:00 p.m.

I rifled through a stack of vintage *National Geographic* magazines. They were stuffed on a shelf in the basement at work, where employees traded unwanted knickknacks. I selected one about deep space and cocked it open with my thumb. Awestruck by the gorgeous, astral mystique of

---

38 Robert Lawrence Kuhn, "Confronting the Multiverse: What 'Infinite Universes' Would Mean," Space.com, December 23, 2015.

39 Ibid.

Creation, I pored over high-resolution imagery of nebulas, moon rocks, black holes, and scintillating hazes of star dust. I pinned the magazine open on a spectacular spread of the Andromeda galaxy, snapped a picture on my phone, and uploaded it to the microcosm of social media.

3:23 p.m.

My phone buzzed. An Instagram message from my sister appeared on screen: three heart-eye emojis.

I smiled. I was surprised. I hadn't spoken to Allie in six months. It was good to hear from her, even if through Instagram. I typed back "Ya girlll. That space life," and sent an emoji of stars. "Send me your address and I'll send you a magazine like this one! There's some free copies here from the archives for the employees."

She sent her address. Then "I miss you immensely."

5:07 p.m.

I stepped from my office building into a shining afternoon. Eric's plane was landing at 6:30 p.m. I dipped into a bodega around the corner and plucked a cheap bottle of champaign from the shelf. A small orange sticker peeled at the edges, reading "$12.99."

5:14 p.m.

I happily carried the bottle in its black, plastic bag to the crosswalk. A small crowd pooled at the street corner ahead. As I approached, a warping awareness absorbed me. The hairs on my arms raised. Time seemed to slow. The sun cast an overwhelmingly sepia tint over everything and I narrowed my eyes. I stood in place and turned my head from side to side, looking for I didn't know what. Leaves spun in an eddy, feeling scripted or choreographed. For Friday rush hour, the sidewalks were uncharacteristically empty.

5:15 p.m.

The crosswalk signal flashed red, and a rapping echoed on the concrete from behind. I turned curiously. A blind woman with long, silver hair, wearing a black dress and black headphones, rushed forward. She swerved in an erratic S shape, expression fearful, like she was fleeing something. She pushed through the crowd and stepped off the curb into the street. It happened so quickly that the group tightened in collective horror as she wound into the intersection.

I lunged forward, caught her by the arm, and pulled her backward as gently as allowed. Her face reflected terror, and she pulled her upper arm from my grip. Panicked, I willed her to remove her headphones, hoping to explain why I grabbed her, but she sped off in the direction that she came from. The crosswalk signal flipped green and the herd crossed, unbothered. I remained in place, confused, heart hammering. I held the champagne bottle limply by the neck.

7:05 p.m.

Boxes drifted about my apartment in towers like sluggish, brown icebergs. I'd moved again and it was my first night in my new home. My new roommate was gone for the weekend, and I was relieved for the solitude to unpack. I propped the back, metal door open with a brick, walked outside, and paced around the driveway while stripping packing tape from empty boxes with a dulling kitchen knife. It was hot and swampy out. Sweat condensed on the nape of my neck. A knee-length dress sucked to the truths of my body, and my hair hung in damp, messy braids.

The sun slipped behind weathervanes and sloping shingles. Streetlights winked on. Leaves hung voltaic green in reflected light over wooden fence panels.

7:21 p.m.

A text from Eric read "Be there in two minutes." I stuffed the sheet of cardboard I was holding into a trash can, and leapt over a flurry of packing peanuts into the kitchen. My stomach rumbled and I removed a slice of leftover pizza from the fridge and stuck it in the microwave. I was hungry, but also needing a prop to steady my hands.

7:23 p.m.

The pizza was twirling glumly on its ceramic plate when a Buick rolled to a stop at the end of the driveway. The windshield was tinted. Eric emerged, and my heart rate quickened. I met him at the back door, gesturing into the apartment with the lukewarm pizza slice.

7:35 p.m.

I flinched as the champagne cork sailed across the alley and it cracked loudly against a neighbor's trash can. We poured two fizzing drinks. Eric took a sip of his, then abandoned the flute on the kitchen counter. "Is it okay if I take a shower?" he asked.

"Sure," I said. "Take your time." I took my glass into the bedroom while I cleared some boxes to make space for his three-day stay.

8:01 p.m.

Eric waddled into my bedroom with a navy-blue towel strung around his waist. He pointed to some insect bites on his midsection. "Got these while camping in the Masai Mara." I reached out, placing my index finger over one of the scars; a little island in a milky sea.

8:04 p.m.

Eric kissed me. I swept a hand behind my back and slid the window curtains closed. "I feel weird," I said, abruptly pulling my face away. "I'm so sorry. I'm not used to this house yet. And now you're here too. And, it's nice, but everything feels really surreal. This whole day feels really *weird*. Do you feel that too? I kind of feel like I'm dreaming."

He kissed me again. "Let's take advantage of that."

9:19 p.m.

A toilet flushed. Eric reappeared from the bathroom.

"I know of a party tonight that I'd like to stop by to see some friends. Would you mind if we go? We don't have to stay long or anything."

9:47 p.m.

We smiled at each other across a table in a Mexican restaurant. Technicolor prisms from a globular light machine affixed to the ceiling swirled across our faces. Music roared from speakers mounted at the corners of the room. The cashier called Eric's name. He retrieved our burritos on a plastic tray from the counter.

10:21 p.m.

I admired the charms of my new neighborhood, like people licking ice cream cones on benches, beside their dogs who lapped out of full, silver water bowls. Ambient notes of indulgence spilled into the street from restaurant doors thrown open. "Okay," Eric said looking at his phone. "I know where we're going. It's one neighborhood over." As we crossed the street, he held my hand for all to see. My belly warmed. *Finally.*

11:06 p.m.

I slid a cold Bud Light can from the torn beer box on the kitchen island. I cracked it open and it fizzed over the aluminum rim. Eric materialized from around a corner with his arm thrown over someone I didn't recognize. "I've been looking for you," he said. He and the friend offered me whiskey from a bottle stowed in the friend's coat pocket. I uncapped the bottle and we each took a swig. Eric introduced me to the person under his arm. I didn't notice whether or not he called me his girlfriend. My throat burned. I wasn't listening.

11:23 p.m.

From the crowded loft, I watched a woman on the floor below, five years my junior, drain shot after shot with puzzling vitality. I yawned and checked my phone for messages. Nothing.

11:54 p.m.

Exhausted, we wrenched our clothes off, slung them onto the floor, and slunk beneath my bedsheets. Two months of pining, our limbs interweaving, we breathed each other in. I sat up to shift my weight and Eric noticed several of his hairs had attached to my chest. We laughed at this and then he kissed me, enmeshing in carnal flashes, pulses racing.

12:22 a.m.

Eric swung his legs over the edge of the bed and ambled into the kitchen. I scooted myself backward against the headboard. Sheets collected in my naked lap and I looked around for my phone. It was glowing on the nightstand. I retrieved it in a long reach. A Facebook message request gleamed on screen from someone named Elora. It read "Call me please. Your sister is at Halifax hospital."

12:32 a.m.

"Okay, thank you," I said, hands shaking. Elora hung up and I dialed the number she gave me to the emergency room. "Hi my sister was just in a motorcycle accident; do you have an Allie there?"

"I don't know," the nurse said. "We just took someone in with no name—a Jane Doe. Let me transfer you to the ICU."

12:44 a.m.

"Hi, yes, we have an Allison," a voice replied. "What's her blood type?"

"I don't know."

"Does she smoke?"

"I don't know."

"Was she pregnant?"

"I don't know."

12:56 a.m.

"She hit her head badly," explained a surgeon in cool, controlled intonations. He detailed the complex domino effects after hitting the ground while not wearing a helmet. "Brain swelling," he stated, conclusively. This was news to me.

1:11 a.m.

I called my mother and my stepmother's cellphones, one by one, impregnated rings. "Allie might be dying. You need to get to the hospital immediately."

1:23 a.m.

I sat on the floor with my back to the wall trembling uncontrollably. Eric walked to the stove, flipped on a burner, and without making a sound, boiled some tea.

1:47 a.m.

The ICU nurse called me back, teary.

"Should I come now?" My hands shook the phone against my ear. "I don't know what to do. I'm a thousand miles away in Washington, DC."

"I don't know what to tell you. She could make it or she could not. We need to wait for her brain to stop swelling." The line went quiet. She lowered her voice. She was crying. "I don't know how to say this, but if this were my sister, I would fly here in a heartbeat."

2:19 a.m.

Eric rubbed my back in the dark. "It's going to be okay," he cooed soothingly. "There's nothing you can do at the moment.

You might as well try to get some sleep. We can figure it out first thing in the morning."

I couldn't see him, but felt his consciousness dimming. His breaths on my neck were warm and thick. *Get some sleep?* I was a humming live wire. My eyes strained open, cast into the dark.

I closed them. When I opened them again my phone was ringing.

2:20 a.m.

The voice of the police chief was low-pitched and resonant. I hung on it as he explained how a man in a pick-up truck, drunk out of his mind, had cut my sister and her boyfriend off while making an illegal U-turn.

"I've been doing this for twenty years. That was the worst accident I've ever seen."

"What do I do?" I begged, weakly.

His honesty was the truest embodiment of mercy. "If you want to say goodbye to her, you need to get your ass on a plane right now. She'll be dead tomorrow before lunchtime."

2:21 a.m.

I stood from the bed and flipped on the lights. "I have to go."

2:32 a.m.

My suitcase was full of books from moving. I dumped them onto the floor and tossed the empty suitcase shell on the bed. All of my clothes were packed up in boxes, except for some miscellaneous things. A black dress with white flowers hung in the closet. I pulled at it, but my hands were shaking too badly. "Which ones do you want?" Eric asked gently. I pointed. He pulled the dress off the hanger for me.

I scrambled around the room, packing anything in my line of sight I might marginally need: socks, a bottle of melatonin, underwear, a journal, a pen, books. I ripped open a cardboard box with clothes inside and yanked out the first two articles my fingers touched. Eric opened my laptop on the bed and searched red eye flights to Florida.

2:38 a.m.

Eric dug through my purse, opened my wallet, and used my credit card to book a ticket at Dulles Airport departing at 4:30 a.m. This gave me ten minutes before I needed to leave the house. While kneeling in front of my bookshelf, a dry sob—more like a bark—cracked out of my mouth. Eric kneeled behind me and rubbed my back. "That's it," he whispered. "You don't have to try to be strong. Let it out." It dawned on me that I hadn't cried since I'd received Elora's text. My eyes screwed up, confused. Rage seared through me. I pulled away from him. *What does* that *mean? I'm not* trying *to* do *anything.*

2:40 a.m.

I rolled my suitcase into the kitchen. "I think I need to drink a glass of water, and sit still for a minute. Then I'll go."

We sat on the couch in the living room side by side, while I took small sips from a water cup. The sink tap echoed a metered drip from the kitchen, and Eric placed his arm around my shoulders. I felt the residue of our sex dried between my thighs underneath my jeans. Eric took my hand and looked at me seriously. "When you get to the airport, you need to be pushy. Tell them you're in an emergency. Ask them to seat you in a row on the plane by yourself." I buried my face in his shoulder and squeezed my eyes closed. I looked at him and responded, "I'm afraid of what I'm going to see."

2:50 a.m.

I pulled my phone out of my purse and balanced it on my thigh as I gunned my car onto the highway. Yellow dashes flicked over the windshield as I dialed. Pacific Standard Time,

Brooke was three hours behind. *Please pick up,* I pleaded. I felt deranged, out of control of my body, like I was not even driving. I needed the ballast of her voice to orient me. When she answered the call, I explained through a cracked voice what was happening. Even though I couldn't cry, she cried for me.

3:47 a.m.

When the airport shuttle pulled up to my dark bus stop and I stepped onto it, the jarring fluorescence of the overhead lighting inversed me. I lifted my suitcase onto a metal rack, took a seat, folded in half, and heaved. The ride lasted for fifteen minutes and I bawled its entirety—a severe, unstoppable, animalistic purge. The shuttle was empty, except for an elderly couple seated across from me. When I looked up from my palms, the wife stood before me. She was clutching the railing with one hand and a fistful of tissues in plastic packaging with the other. I took the tissues from her and thanked her with my dripping face. Consumed by extraordinary agony, the softness of meager kindnesses felt saint like, otherworldly.

4:19 a.m.

My face was already swelling from the overrunning of tears that had become irrepressible, exacerbated by lack of sleep. I bolted across the airport hangar to the gate, but when I got there the clerks were sealing off the gate door. Hysterical, I threw myself on the counter. Spit dripped from my lips, I clenched the used tissues in my fist, and begged, "please let me on. My sister is *dying*."

4:55 a.m.

I laid across all of the seats in row three. I closed my eyes, and tried to steady my breathing. The plane was nearly empty.

6:03 a.m.

Held by the sky, I experienced a dreamlike equanimity. Or maybe it wasn't calm, but *trust.* I knew the airplane would deliver me to where I needed to be. Among precipitous unknowns, any certainty was luxury. Stilled in the liminal, I eyed the AC nozzles hissing in the ceiling. Evidence of morning streaked the sky.

7:23 a.m.

The clerk behind the rental car counter demanded I show proof of insurance. "I don't have it with me!" I shouted hoarsely. "Please, I need a car so I can get to the hospital." He rolled his eyes and disappeared into a back room. A manager shuffled out to handle me. Smooth as silk, he slipped me paper after paper and I agreed to whatever he presented, weaving my signature on every line. I tossed my credit card onto the counter like it was nothing.

9:14 a.m.

When I stepped out of the rental car into the hospital parking lot, the daylight arrested me. The air smelled of salt water and swamp reeds. I looked down at myself, alarmed at the garments I'd blindly selected for the event of my sister's death: acid washed skinny jeans and a thin, yellow, fast fashion T-shirt. Both were three sizes too small. Neither had been worn in years. I fretfully pulled the T-shirt down so that it covered my belly button, but it sprung up to my ribcage. My obliques bulged over the waistline of the jeans.

9:26 a.m.

I passed through hospital security and saw my grandpa pacing at the end of the hall. He turned, read my face, and smiled sympathetically. I wrapped my arms around my naked midriff and shivered. He pulled off his extra-large, forest green windbreaker and cloaked me in it.

• • •

When Allie hit the ground, her heart stopped. Five minutes passed before EMTs were able to resuscitate her. When she came back to life, her blood pressure was in hypotension. Paramedics intubated her in the ambulance and, in doing so, noted she demonstrated no gag reflex, sign of motor function, or response to painful stimuli. The intubater connected to a machine ventilator that pumped air and blood to her vital organs because her heart was too weak to do so on its own.

Her lung was punctured and air rushed into it, building pressure. In the emergency room, they routed a pneumothorax tube into her chest to remove the excess air. No neurosurgeon was on staff at the time she was admitted, so one was called in from home at 11:50 p.m. It took him twenty-three minutes to arrive. In the meantime, a rapid infusion line was inserted into her left subclavian vein, near her clavicle, to infuse medication into her blood stream as quickly as possible.

From the moment I stepped into her room in the intensive care unit, I observed Allie in a transforming sequence of shock. Our first moments together, I took her in emotionless and vacant.

I made her out between wires and tubes that were woven through her hospital gown, taped to her fingers, to her arms, down her throat, into her chest. Her eyes were closed and the lids were blackened and convex, like ripened avocados. Her face, lips, and fingers were swelled to an extent that they did not look like lips or fingers any longer. Her hair matted with blood at the back of her head and dried to the sheets.

Earlier in the morning, they'd rolled her in for a CT scan. The scan showed severe traumatic brain injury and multiple skull fractures of the occipital bone, located toward the back of her head. She had traumatic subarachnoid hemorrhaging, meaning the area between her brain and the tissue covering the brain was bleeding. In addition to the puncture, she had fluid in her lungs.

After the CT scan, they'd drilled holes into her skull, placing bolts at her temples that secured an inter-cranial pressure monitor, which measures pressure in the skull from brain bleed.

Diagnosis: Current massive brain trauma. Condition nonreversible.

• • •

Allie had opted on her driver's license to donate her organs. After the CT scan, the organ donation team was called. The ICU nurses were instructed to keep Allie's body alive long enough until a surgeon could come in the next few days to extract her viable organs.

On my second day in the hospital, I followed my mother's lead. A nurse rolled a cart into Allie's room that was stocked with clean, white rags. We filled Styrofoam cups with water and warmed them in the microwave. I helped Mom dip the rags into the water, and wipe blood that leaked from Allie's ears, nose, and mouth, as her brain continued to swell and her body changed shape. She used a tube, like at the dentist, to suck out the spittle and dried blood that collected in Allie's mouth, which was propped open. She applied Vaseline to Allie's lips, which were dried and blistering. "The swelling should be going down soon," she said tenderly.

Little by little, Allie's natural colors and shapes restored. The mechanical ventilator that pumped air into her lungs created an illusion of breathing, of aliveness. At first, I was afraid to get too close to her. To touch her even. When we were alone, I smoothed my index finger over the back of her hand. Then held her warm, soft fingertips in mine. I wiped her ears with warm wash cloths. I tried to feel her there with me, not in her body, but in the air.

Eventually, I caught on to the multiverse's idiosyncrasies—its expansion and contraction of time. Dusk blurred into night and dawn blurred into day. I refused to abandon Allie by leaving the hospital. Instead, I swished around her room and through the corridors endlessly in the enormous, green windbreaker. Overnight, Mom and I slept in a small, empty conference room down the hall. She curled up on a bench and I laid on the floor, using the balled-up windbreaker as a pillow. While the ICU was peaceful during the day, at night it was cacophonous because that's when they did surgeries. Trapped in a waking nightmare, resting on concrete, I drifted in and out of consciousness to the radical discord of drilling.

• • •

On the third day I was everything.

A reporter on the scene, I scribbled furious notes in my journal of who came into the room, what they said, what they wore, their organizational affiliation, what time it was, how I was feeling. I wasn't sure why, but my illegible, frenetic record keeping asserted to the forefront of my priorities. Between shock and mania, I could no longer hold the unending particulars, occurring moment to moment, that overflowed the trap of my mind.

A host, open and approachable, I welcomed Allie's visitors into her hospital room. Some were timid, having never met her family. Like a politician, I embraced them, shook their hands, gave them space, invited them to write cherished memories of Allie down on a scroll of paper with an orange highlighter—a paper I hung across some cabinets for all to see.

A speech writer, I squatted low over a sheet of notebook paper on the coffee table in the conference room, surrounded by a semicircle made up of nodding family members and the organ donation proctor. I scripted a prayer, composed of suggestions by the group, that the organ donation surgeon would ceremoniously read.

An event coordinator, I marched up and down the hospital halls, volleying voicemails back and forth to my mother's church on whether the recreation room would be available for a reception in the coming week.

A correspondent, I reported hourly status updates via text and phone calls to my stepmother and father's side of the family.

A martyr, I tumbled into Allie's hospital room gasping and, between panic-stricken breaths, cried, "I need help! I can't do it all by myself!" My aunt took me outside for air and said, "Nicki, we can help you. It just seems really important to you to be in charge of everything."

My mother's reaction to sudden death, to losing her child, was despondence—a slow, deceleration into sorrow. My reaction was desperation—an acceleration into despair. A true perfectionist, if I could take care of every single errand, perform perfectly in every role, maybe that would *earn* us something. If I could be involved in every aspect of Allie's death, maybe I could keep her essence alive on me a little longer. Maybe she would know how much she meant to me, maybe I could prove my relevance to her. If I kept moving, kept managing, kept controlling, I wouldn't have to sit back in the bedside recliner and watch her die.

• • •

In the multiverse, titles and hierarchies rearrange. Surgeons were not surgeons, but priests. Nurses were not nurses, but powder blue seraphs. They spoke to me like sisters, paragons of benevolence and decency. Nurses held my hand, rubbed my back, wept for my family.

On the fourth day I emptied.

During the first minute I was alone with my father in Allie's hospital room, two nurses trickled in. They opened and closed drawers, fiddled with utensils, glanced cautiously over at me. I knew what they were doing. They didn't need to speak. On the fifth minute, I rose stiffly from my chair, walked out of the room, called my friend Abbie, and collapsed on a marble staircase down the hall. Abbie, who was staying at her parent's house in Ormond Beach, flew to the hospital like my guardian angel in ten minutes flat. She and my cousin picked me up, and dragged me, wailing, to my feet. Rivaling the Madonna and Child, on the carpet of the empty hospital chapel, Abbie cradled my curled body that draped over her lap.

An hour later, my mom, stepdad, niece, and I slumped around Allie's room in dull, flickering lights. We watched a clock ticking over the doorway, counting the hours until the organ donation team was scheduled to show. Nurses popped in every so often to report the team had again pushed their arrival back, adding an hour or two to the wait. Time slowed so much so its passage was undetectable. It was dark outside, but I didn't know if it was six o'clock in the morning or six o'clock at night.

In our last moments with Allie's warm, corporeal form, my mother, stepfather, niece, and grandparents formed a ring around Allie's hospital bed holding hands. Tears streamed over our cheeks and down the necks of our shirts as we blurted out our loveliest recollections.

The organ donation surgeon entered the room, clutching the notebook paper prayer I'd scratched out in his meaty fist.

We swallowed him into the circle and he cried too as he read the prayer aloud. Afterward, for one whole minute, he raised an electronic device to Allie's chest that amplified the sound of her heartbeat. Tightening our ring, cellphones extended, we relied on the benevolence of technology to capture her final traces.

17

GEOLOGY

The last time I saw Allie in person was on Christmas Day in 2016, while I was visiting home from DC. Allie had just given birth to a son. She, her partner, and the baby attended Mom's house specifically to see Allie's daughter, but also the rest of the family. I was quietly overjoyed. They stayed through the evening, and pulled up chairs to the dinner table. I swaddled my nephew against my chest.

Allie was looking much better than she had in the previous years I'd seen her. Her complexion was full and bright. She was light and charming, calm and responsible. She'd just been promoted as a training manager for the restaurant chain she worked for, was traveling around the country, and had rented her very own apartment. She was figuring things out, just like me.

After dinner, when they were getting ready to leave, she squeezed everyone in the room, especially my niece. When I hugged her goodbye, she whispered into my ear "I love you."

"I love you too," I whispered, gladly.

When we released, she was teary eyed and smiling.

• • •

While shopping for Allie's casket clothing with my mom in the days after her death, I broke down in the middle of a department store as a panic attack swept over me. The multiverse wasn't done with us yet.

Before the funeral, the priest warned us about reading our own eulogies. "The family becomes too emotional once the day arrives and can't get through it." Still, I remained dedicated to reading my own eulogy. I wasn't sure if Allie was even religious, and the thought of a priest delivering a canned oration didn't feel right. I didn't know Allie as closely as her friends knew her when she died, but I'd known her during the shaping of her foundation. So I wrote through this lens.

On the day of the funeral, my mother delivered her speech before mine. But when she stepped up to the microphone she shattered into pieces. I was nicked by the shards of her voice, and started to crack open too. When she finished speaking and took a step backward, I collected her in my arms, holding her tightly on stage as one hundred eyes held us.

When it was my turn to read, the opposite happened. A job to be done, my feelings cleared me. I felt spontaneous warmth recounting our childhood and the impression my sister left on me. My lightness may have even felt inappropriate because it surprised me too. The automation of my compartmentalization was startling.

The procession out of the church was a different story. The trumpets blared and pallbearers vaulted the casket into the air. The march up the aisle began and I blacked out. My legs wouldn't work—I couldn't walk. Exploding into a deluge of sobs, I don't know how it happened exactly, but I was dragged up the aisle by the collective. My arms were woven over shoulders and around other arms. My toes pointed downward and the tops of my feet skated across the carpet. As if downed into the throat of a monster, together we moved forward.

Over the thunderous horns, my heart slamming in my ears, the visual overwhelm, the faces in pews leering, the lambasting of my immediacy—I could not break free. My stepmother leaned in from somewhere behind and whispered into my ear clear as crystal, "You're the star now."

• • •

My grief was all of me, and all of me felt like a boulder whose insides were divided by geological stratum. There was a grief layer for the remainder of Allie's life she would never get to see. A grief layer for her children. Below that, a grief layer for our stolen, future memories. Below that, a particularly thick grief layer for the loss of our shared history. The only person who understood the explicit difficulties of my childhood, from the lens I experienced it through, had vanished forever. This was a special type of *alone.*

My grief taught me the benefits of simplicity. The questions I valued the most were monosyllabic, like "do you need to eat?"

I received overwhelming generosities in the wake of my sister's death—a type of altruism I was unfamiliar with. I was impressed upon by what felt like exorbitant kindness—my perspective on humanity's collective goodness brightened and deepened. From all sorts of unexpected origins, friends and family donated their time, money, emotional support, or all three. Some sent cards. Some sent flowers. Some drove great distances. Some talked to me on the phone whenever I wanted. Some bowed over like reeds in a wicked storm, forming a path to help brave the course ahead.

I straddled a crevasse with one foothold in suffering and the other in love. A confusion of heavy and light.

I was warmed, and yet I stung all over. All hurt was exaggerated, and some people said truly thoughtless things. Some made my grief about themselves by trying to fix it. Others tried to commiserate by referencing the deaths of their grandparents or pets, as if these were at all comparable. To keep sanity abreast in the enormous shadow of Allie's sudden death, I tried my hardest to parse condolences for their intentions rather than their content. Still, I was outraged despite well-meaning.

I barely cried for two weeks. A few times I drove to a field near my mom's house, where I used to smoke cigarettes in college, and tried to muster any tears at all. Nothing came. Instead of crying, I thought about selfish things. Watching tall grass ripple in the wind through the windshield of my car, I asked *Why hasn't Eric called? Where is he?* For thinking about anything besides Allie, I felt guilty and disturbed.

When the bad feelings did come, they presented in panic attacks that swallowed me whole—surges of hysteria that rushed forward. Usually occurring at night, and while alone, my mind went black. I tumbled into a tunnel, a feeling of total detachment and separateness from the present. I woke up in the middle of the night gasping from nightmares. My memory returned to my sister's face inside of her coffin, waxy and so unlike her own.

Perplexed, I couldn't make my mind understand the impossible, mysterious transition of a human body turning from animate and kinetic to defunct, carbon ash. It wasn't a misunderstanding of science or physics—a conundrum of the heart, not the mind.

In my therapist's office I cried, "I'm scared of remembering Allie only how she looked on her deathbed."

"When the grief comes," Ramona said, "try to think about happy things."

I glared at her. *That's stupid,* I thought. *Don't you understand the magnitude of what I've seen?*

In a way, I also didn't want to forget. I had witnessed something important and profound. The capacity of death would critically inform the rest of my life, introducing radical clarity.

• • •

After a week back in my DC apartment, something I'd completely forgotten flew into my mind. Right before Allie's death, on a whim, I'd purchased round-trip tickets to Colorado Springs.

I'd only been at my job for three months, and had already taken two weeks of bereavement leave. But when I went into the office the next day, I asked my new boss if I could take an additional week off.

"Weren't you just out for two weeks?" he asked rhetorically.

My mouth dried. "Yes... but there was a lot to be done during that time. I had no time to grieve."

Later that day, I asked Ramona, "Do you think I should go? I'm scared that I'll be fired, but I really need some time to myself." I wrung my hands in my lap.

She furrowed her brow, like I asked her something crazy. "*Go,*" she said confidently. "If you need a doctor's note for work, I will write you one myself."

I got on the plane a week later. When it touched down at the airport, I met up with an incredible friend with a heart of solid gold. She offered me her car, her camping gear, and her sandals. Then I drove one thousand miles across Colorado.

• • •

The first place I drove to in the 2001 Mitsubishi Lancer was the Great Sand Dunes National Park, but I stopped at Kentucky Fried Chicken on the way. Hurtling through the heat of the desert, I ripped chicken skin from bone with my fangs. Grease coated my cheeks.

Approaching the park at dusk, sand dunes the size of buildings loomed in the distance. A backdrop of snowcapped mountains pierced the sky. I set up the tent and took a walk to the dune field to watch the sunset, where the sand met the atmosphere. I placed one sandaled foot on the base of a dune and started climbing. The surface was tougher in places than I expected, but I was reminded of my youth at the beach—Allie and I taking turns clumsily carrying folding chairs, umbrellas, boogie boards, coolers, and plastic buckets over the beach dunes to Mom's van after sun-kissed days at the ocean.

I reached a dune peak, three-hundred feet high, and took a seat. Hikers below were so distant they were inscrutable. It was silent and I remained completely still, becoming part of the landscape. Then I rocked backward, inhaled, and screamed. Insulated by distance and carried off by the wind, no one could hear me. I did it again. My voice vibrated in my chest and I realized my whole insides were jam packed with yells.

I'd read that, using Optically-Stimulated Luminescence, samples from inside the dunes could be tested for age based on how long the quartz grains were buried in darkness. Some deposits dated seven hundred and fifty years old, blown in during a drought, while other deposits dated eighteen thousand years old—toward the last ice age.[40] The dune peaks were interconnected by phantasmic weaving, snakelike whispers

---

40 "Sand Dunes: Geology," National Park Service, accessed March 4, 2021.

of sand, circling pockets sixty feet wide and sixty feet deep. The park brochures hadn't mentioned anything about spirits, but I definitely saw them blowing around in translucent sheets—huge, swirling bodies of dust. The longer I sat, the fiercer the wind became, at thirty-mile-per-hour gusts. It was time for me to leave.

I descended from my perch, running, sliding, and sinking into the slope until I reached the flat plane of the ground. I spun on my heel to examine the setting sun one last time, walking slowly backward.

The sky, from top to bottom, turned from navy to pink to orange to yellow. The crescent moon hung tethered by a silk string. Tears skidded my cheeks from my lower lids and remained frozen there like tiny beads of fire stinging in the wind. Night hikers started an ascent in the distance, looking like glow bugs, headlamps bobbing. I lowered to my knees and sat back on my foot heels. My fingertips raked the dirt. I looked around. No one else in sight—not in all the rippling acreage of beige that stretched into a coal-colored dusk.

Then the wind knocked my ball cap to the ground. It was bright pink with a red lobster sewn onto the front. It looked appropriately nestled in the sand. *Finally, the lobster in its natural habitat,* I thought.

By the time I made it back to my campsite it was dark. I unzipped the door of the tent, slipped into the sleeping bag, and gazed unobstructed by the mesh ceiling into a combustion of stars. They were mesmerizing, just like in the *National Geographic* magazine.

My therapist had lent me a book called *Writing to Heal the Soul: Transforming Grief and Loss Through Writing.* I pictured it mashed at the bottom of my backpack which was locked in the trunk. While I'd planned to spend a significant portion of the trip writing about death to help myself process, the truth was I didn't feel much like writing about death *or* about the beauty I was seeing. I much preferred being present in the moment—screaming into the sun like a lunatic, eating fried chicken, and pioneering the sky with my eyes. I wondered if I was doing the work of processing death just by being exactly where I was in the all-encompassing wisdom of the natural world. By standing still on ancient sand, forever rearranging.

• • •

I accepted early on the tent would never make it back inside its original packaging—not without sorcery. I stuffed it into the trunk with flat, stiff hands. I would manage in an organized chaos. I deemed the passenger seat fit for art supplies and expensive papers, the trunk for camp equipment, and the back seat for my explosion of clothing.

Before the next leg of the drive, I rifled through CDs in the driver's side door pocket. I found a Beatles Anthology, inserted it into the stereo, and reentered the highway coursing through the arid desert. When a cover of *My Bonnie Lies Over the Ocean* came on, I stiffened. I was transported. The morning after Allie's funeral, I'd sat on the beach at sunrise humming this song as I painted. Except I'd changed the word Bonnie to *body. My body lies over the ocean.* I kept picturing the painting *The Castle of the Pyrenees* by surrealist Rene Magritte as I hummed, which depicted a gigantic rock levitating over the sea, heavy and light.

I drove four and half hours through the afternoon until evening. I pitched my tent in the center of a field at the top of a mesa in Mesa Verde National Park. At 3:00 a.m., I awoke to fortuitous cracks of lightning. The mesa was at 7,800 feet, and the bolts were eye level. I ran across the field and huddled beneath a bathroom overhang. Exhausted, I tried to reason *is it safer to sleep in the middle of the field or in my metal car? I'm safe in the car because of the rubber tires, right? Isn't that a thing? Maybe I could sleep in the bathroom.* I peeked into the bathroom. It was small. *I could make an "out of order" sign, tape it to the stall, then sleep on the floor. Which end would my head go? I guess I'd have to lay it next to the toilet, and my feet would probably stick out from underneath the door.* A bat swooped in front of my face, clapped down on a moth the size of a fist, and disappeared into the night.

I slept in the car.

• • •

The next morning, the sky was lavender, garnished with wispy pink clouds. I treaded into the field to find the storm had blown the tent into a pathetic, wet heap. I pulled apart the poles and folded up the wet materials.

At the camp store, I treated myself to a coffee. I took it with me into an adjacent building where I purchased a hot shower with the quarters at the bottom of my backpack. The shower tiles were mealy, dismantled, and falling out of place. A sign was fastened on the wall showing a silhouetted figure defecating on the floor, covered by a big, red X. And yet, I felt like a queen. I stripped off my leggings and sand sprinkled to the floor, forming a miniature dune. I scrubbed belligerently around my alcoves and raked conditioner squirted from mini bottles through my greasy, tangled hair.

After the shower, I clutched the coffee in the front seat of the car, shivering. It was raining again and thirty degrees. The fickleness of the weather was tiresome because the car didn't have a defroster. If I turned on the heat, a film developed on the interior of the windshield that I repeatedly wiped away with my hand, by leaning over the steering wheel.

I drove to an overlook, pulled on my friend's snow jacket, and walked to the railing. My hands were freezing, even wrapped around the scorching cup of bean water, but the unfolding canyon was stunning. Buttes, plateaus, and flat-headed rocks stretched wide into downward slopes, reaching into valleys. A plaque described how the land of Mesa Verde is continuously shaped by wildfires from lightning, which frequently strikes the ground.

Cumulonimbus clouds loomed in the distance. Another lightning storm was approaching and I jogged back to the car. As I zigzagged out of the park, the sky blackened, and I passed entire groves of piñon and juniper that were charred and scorched. Fueled by the grim scenery, frustration rose to the surface of my contemplations. I thought about spats I had in my friendships since Allie died, and the inability of some people, who's opinions I cared about, to validate me.

I didn't know anyone who had witnessed the severity of what I had at my age. Who could I talk to about it? Who would really understand? *Will I ever meet anyone who will love me including these difficult experiences I carry?*

• • •

The bordering towns beyond Mesa Verde, leading into San Juan National Forest, were drab and lifeless, and the weather was getting to me. My mind drifted to a prompt in the grief book I'd been skipping over. It was, "Imagine your own death and write about how you lived up until that moment. Are you comfortable with the choices you made?"[41] Allie's death

41 Susan Zimmermann, *Writing to Heal the Soul: Transforming Grief and Loss Through Writing* (New York: The Crown Publishing Group, 2002), 50.

showed me how close we all are all the time to our mortality, and I didn't want to look at this. It gave me anxiety, which I met with avoidance.

Mountains cropped up along either side of the road. I plunged into the depths of 1.8 million acres of forest.

I'd listened to all the CDs in the car door, so I pulled out my headphones and played some music stored on my phone by Kevin Morby. I rolled the windows down halfway and brisk, fall air rushed in. With the music turned up loudly, I couldn't hear myself singing, but realized toward the end of the first song that I was actually yelling. Extravagant mounds of yellow and green scrolled the panorama.

I accelerated. The next song that ticked on was called "Pearly Gates." I never minded this song before, but it quickly took on new meaning. In it, Kevin describes what his own funeral might be like some day. Its onset seemed uncomfortably coincidental. An aftershock, the multiverse was lurching again. The temperature started dropping, but I kept the windows rolled down. My knuckles burned and my breath turned into visible plumes.

The windows fogged from the heat of my body. I rolled them down even more to clear them and snowflakes flurried in. I stretched into the back seat for a paper towel to wipe the inside of the fogging windshield with. When I did, I smelled iron and felt warmth above my upper lip. I dabbed at it with the paper towel roll and it printed with vibrant red crescents.

I smudged the paper towels against the windshield, and through a translucent smear, noticed a dainty, silver camper parked at the base of a mountain. Beside that, a flock of two hundred sheep. Intrigued and wonderstruck, I spotted a gravel patch up ahead and whipped into it. I threw the car into park, rolled up the windows, and laced up my boots.

Through the windshield, a sign marked a trailhead, "Cross Trail," that led to a small body of water, "Priest Lake." The multiverse had routed me into a live parable.

I stepped from the car and sunk into cold clay. Up the hill was the silhouette of a sheepherder, who presumably lived in the silver camper. A sheepdog with loose, flowing locks danced beside him. The sheepherder, an intermediary, was no threat to me, nor I to him, and we made this assessment of each other wordlessly. The sheep were skeptical. They formed tidy lines, streaming up the mountain. Skittish at my slow approach, they sounded a chorus of collective bleats. Tagged with blue spots on their wool, I was envious in all the cold at their lush coats.

Amused, I trotted alongside the tail end of their company. Eventually they scuttled farther up the mountain than I cared to go and the sheepherder and his companion disappeared into the snowfall-like apparitions. The whole scene seemed illusory, especially through an alabaster haze.

When the last of the sheep vanished beyond my view, I trekked back toward the gravel lot. My boots crunched over ice and I stepped delicately over a wooden bridge that curved over a small creek. I looked out at the pass. The whiteout enveloped everything. This chimerical afterlife was nice, at least. Daydreaming, my attention left my extremities. When it returned a few minutes later, I noticed they no longer ached with cold. My whole body felt airy and painless. I felt at peace.

18

PROXIMITY

Before ending my drive through Colorado in Denver, I passed through Telluride first. I wasn't equipped to camp in the snowstorm, so I booked the only place I could find for two nights, which happened to be a too-expensive one-bedroom townhome. I dragged my suitcase and art supplies inside. The rooms were clean and noiseless. I laid in the luxury bed, closed my eyes, and relaxed. Missing the comfort of Eric's voice, I picked up my phone and texted him. He responded immediately. He couldn't talk. He was out in Brooklyn partying with friends.

I flew back to DC a few days later. When Eric visited me next, in early October 2017, it had been only a little over month since I'd last seen him, but the multiverse had changed us. I was no longer me and he was no longer him.

He showed up to my apartment at five o'clock on Friday evening, smiling and buzzed. My superpowers detected something was amiss. He requested we go out drinking at 7:00 p.m. with such a confidence that I questioned if I were odd for wanting to stay in. At 7:00 p.m., I faced the closet, glowered, and tucked a blouse into my jeans. Uncharacteristically jovial, he floated around the kitchen while waiting for me to apply my makeup. I uncapped my eyeliner pencil and drew a perfect line across each eyelid. I sat back, looked at myself in the mirror, and felt nauseated. *What are you doing?* I asked myself. *What the hell are you celebrating for?*

I burst into tears, thrown by an combination of guilt and sadness. I stayed home that night and Eric went out without me.

On Sunday morning, before Eric was set to catch his train back to Connecticut, I laid in bed with a total lack of energy. He wrinkled his nose at me while he packed his things.

"Aren't you going to get up and *do* something today?"

I was embarrassed by the question. "I don't know," I mumbled. "I feel really depressed." My eyes burned with the promise of tears.

"Well, you'd probably feel better if you got up and *did* something with yourself." I buried my face in my pillow and cried. He left without hugging me goodbye.

Later that night, from the burrow of my sheets, I picked up my phone and tapped out the question I already knew the answer to.

"Did you sleep with someone else?" My finger hovered over the send button. My hands were trembling.

Sent.

A speech bubble percolated. Then nothing. Then percolated. Then nothing.

The truth appeared.

"Yes."

"When?"

"About two weeks after you left for Florida."

To be hurt in this specific way, during this specific time, from this specific person who had witnessed the worst night of my life, was a specific type of devastating. Still, I struggled to fully separate from Eric in the months that followed. He begged for forgiveness, explaining he'd been physically ill after he'd done it and how wrecked with guilt he was. We sent verbose and heated emails, took breaks to gather our thoughts, changed our minds back and forth. October transitioned to November and then December. Each week, he asked, "are you ready to try again?" My mind wanted to say yes, but my body was undeniably no. Our moment had eclipsed. It was frozen behind us in the umbra. Eventually, we left it there.

• • •

Every day I woke up at 8:00 a.m., dressed myself, and went to work. I spoke with colleagues normally, as if I hadn't just witnessed someone brutally die in front of me. On top of everything, bizarre text messages from my father cropped up increasingly—belligerent accusations that I didn't understand. On my way into meetings, I glanced down at notifications on my phone that read "watch your back," or "you're making enemies."

One day, I screenshot a particularly detailed message from him and forwarded it to Brooke. "I can't handle this anymore," I captioned it. "I just had to present mock-ups of my work to the entire marketing team directly after receiving this."

She said, "You need to block him, Nicki. This isn't good for you."

A year earlier, I'd given him an ultimatum. "I can no longer have a relationship with you," I wrote, "if you cannot treat me respectfully, like fathers are supposed to treat their children. I need you to be supportive, loving, and calm." This was the most direct I'd ever been with him. To this, we met in a transformative place. "I can't do that," he replied. "That's not *me*."

While profoundly disappointing, this was an invitation to liberation. Through frankness, my father handed me a reckoning.

After this, we had mostly stopped speaking, but at Allie's funeral reception he'd cornered me hovering over me with tears in his eyes. "How much longer will you go without speaking to me? A year? Five years? How much time are you willing to *waste*?" I was overwhelmed by the confrontation and pulled away, but I was not unaffected.

Retreating from pain, like jerking a hand away from fire, is instinctual, and yet for twenty-seven years I continuously scorched myself by placing my hand on the blaze of my father. I liken my experience to Tara Westover's in her memoir *Educated*. Throughout the novel, tension builds as Tara endures her family who abuses her, sabotages her, and gaslights her. She emancipates herself using higher education, but the reader is brought to frustration by her inability to quit her family entirely.[42] Contrarily, I was not confused by Tara's family dynamic. I *got* Tara. I understood the draw to her father because I had the draw too.

While most stories are simplified through archetypes, it would've been easy to conclude mine, to separate from my father permanently by making him into a villain. However, when I pulled my life story apart like an accordion, he had played many roles. At times, he'd been an outlaw and an explorer. He'd been an everyman and a jester. He'd even been a hero.

Research conducted on nonhuman mammals concludes that, no matter the conditions of the nests we are born into,

---

42 Tara Westover, *Educated* (New York City: Penguin Random House LLC., 2018), 313.

we are wired to return to them.[43] Even if we experience more pleasant surroundings after we leave, and especially during times of stress, we return. Returning isn't ineptitude, it's biology. Because the intense pull to my father has not lessened over thirty-one years, I am faced with accepting the draw will never leave me. My hunger to restore our relationship is a birthmark, a fundamental priming.

That being said, humans possess free will and higher intelligence. As his threats rolled in, I weighed my options carefully. I could continue oscillating between my desires that he would one day change and my disappointments when he hadn't. Or I could learn to ultimately accept him as he was, without necessarily putting myself in the way of mistreatment. I could try to love him at a distance.

Leaning against a wall in the women's restroom at work, I peered at Brooke's text, reading and rereading it. I decided to act, not out of spite or valiance, but out of sheer curiosity. I wondered what would happen if I did what was counter to what I knew. *I wonder what will happen if I stop attending to his feelings and start attending to my own?*

Like in Tara's story, when I stopped speaking to my dad or allowing his calls or text messages to reach me, for I didn't know how long, the initial enforcement of my boundary didn't stop at him. Like a lens flare, he was at the center and a safeguard orbited him like a halo. Relatives encouraged me to call or put myself in environments where I was accessible to him. At first, I felt flustered by these pressures. I tried to explain and defend myself in verbose messages that read unintelligibly.

---

43 Bessel Van Der Kolk, *The Body Keeps the Score: Brain, Mind, and Body in the Healing of Trauma* (New York: Penguin Books, 2015), 31.

Then I gave up explaining. Pushed to capacity, my system was overloading. I set a second boundary, this time not against specific people, but against the sensation of pain itself. At the seat of my inner circuit breaker, anyone introducing pain into my life had to be switched off immediately.

• • •

In the passage of quietude between us, I realized I didn't need to reset my relationship *with* my father, but *to* my father.

While I depended on him in childhood for security, nourishment, and belonging, I discovered in adulthood the draw to him was actually *fear.* I feared long-term space would reap unbearable consequences and that a complete separation from either of my parents would destroy me, as if we were one, and being separated would rip us into halves. The fear told me if I challenged or separated from my parents, I risked being outcast from my extended family too.

Sometimes what we fear the most is what we actually need. It was impossible to heal from my relationship with my father while still being active in it. The space allowed me to reorganize my understanding of things, to develop an exclusive sense of self, and to step into my truest adulthood.

While I couldn't control what I was subjected to in childhood, I learned that I can control how I react to the former subjections. Like a porter, I carried the hefty impacts of my trauma for twenty-seven years, I even rolled it into my identity. After years of therapy and self-work, I learned to set down some of my haul. I found that compassion and forgiveness are easier to carry than resentment and blame. *Time is of the essence. How am I going to be?*

In my mind and my memories, I've rebranded my father yet again a different archetype. Today, I see him as a teacher, as his nature showed me where I can soften and where I can strengthen. He showed me the extent of behaviors I was willing to accept from others. He is a benchmark of where I have come from that informs me of where I'd like to go.

Instead of turning to my father for security, nourishment, approval, and belonging, I have learned to turn to myself.

• • •

Ramona said something surprising to me once.

"I notice that when you cry you cover your face with your hands. Adults and children tend to express their emotions differently. The way you place your fingers over your eyes is very childlike." She demonstrated.

In essence, she told me I cry like a baby.

One night while reading in my bedroom, from the depths of a lull, I felt it impending. A lethal combination: The Dread plus grief. Its tingles welled up in me. My limbic brain screened the sensations and transmitted the emergency code to my reptilian brain. I sat up and panicked. Sirens sounded. My body prepared for a tsunami.

Whenever I sensed an onset of bad feelings, I picked up my phone and I called someone. My friends were all emergency contacts—jet skis that I hopped on to peel away from emotional swells. I sifted my mind for people or group chats to text or enter to ease the blow of the forthcoming calamity.

Who can I call? I raised my cell phone to my chest and gazed into its black screen. Before I could decide, it was too late. The tsunami struck. I dropped the phone and flopped backward into a pile of laundry shaped like a volcano. For twenty uninterrupted minutes I cried. I bawled, I moaned, and rolled from side to side. Like a child, I sucked in shuddering breaths. I let myself feel everything.

Finally, I stood up and moped into the kitchen. I put a pot of water on the stove and turned the dial. When the water finished boiling, I poured it into a mug, added a tea bag, and carried it back into my bedroom. I sniffled and studied the laundry explosion on the bed, a human-sized impression caved in the center. I set the tea down on the nightstand, picked up a pair of underwear, and folded it into a triangle. I sniffled again and folded another pair. Then I folded a pair of jeans. By the time I reconstructed the laundry explosion into a series of pueblo-like stacks, I looked up and gasped. *I just regulated my own feelings.*

I had heard the phrase "regulate your emotions" thrown around before and I thought I knew what it meant, but I didn't. Not until I learned through practice that the force of my fear, anger, and sadness would not kill me. While having my bad feelings, I stopped stuffing, distracting, or redirecting them by scrolling on my phone, drinking, or pulling out my hair. I allowed them to surge me like a tide. I survived.

Toward the end of December, on my twenty-eighth birthday, while home visiting family, my mom handed me a small, shiny package. I unwrapped the paper and opened the box. Inside was a silver ring in the shape of a wave. I pinched the ring away from the white stuffing and slid it over my middle finger. "I bought one for myself too," said my mom. "You know. To remind us of the temporariness of ups and downs in life." To remind me I didn't have to run from myself anymore. To remind me I wasn't just the boulder, I was also the ocean.

19

EXPANSION

I found myself typing repetitious Google searches like "how long does the grieving process take?" The results provided familiar rhetoric; "everyone's timeline is different." Or conflicting blog posts that either stated "it takes three years," or "it takes five years." I stumbled across sites that warned against "complicated grief"—grief that persevered beyond its expiration date, suggesting there was one. Still, I searched. It wasn't the answers, but the act of searching that gave me a sense of control.

I initiated new rituals and, each night, tried my best to transfer all my questions into a notebook. Sometimes I used the prompts from my *Writing Through Grief* book, and sometimes I did not. Either way, transferring my pain onto paper helped it make a little more sense. Or at least made me a little less dense.

My new rent was cheap, and because I laid low all winter I found that I had done an impressive job of repairing my financial state. I had paid off most of my credit card debt, and even managed to even save $10,000, which was more money than I'd ever had in my life. A calling swept through me again, the same type of calling that lured me to California. I craved a bodily and intellectual expansion. I needed something to look forward to. I needed *movement.* This time bigger, farther, and longer.

In early April 2018, I opened my laptop and searched flights to Europe. Moments later, I purchased myself a one-way ticket to Paris in August—a year anniversary since Allie's death. Then I purchased a ticket to Lisbon from Paris. Then a ticket to Reykjavik from Lisbon. Again, I had no idea what I was doing, or how to prepare, but I was building trust with myself. I chose to believe, when the time came, I could depend on myself to give me what I needed.

• • •

I stayed in France, Portugal, and Iceland for about six days each. Like the first time I traveled alone, I was timid at first, except this time I was separated from home by an ocean. I'd been too cheap to pay for overseas cell signal and planned to navigate across Europe relying on public Wi-Fi, city maps, or—with remarkable confidence—the kindness of strangers.

I'd spent the prior three months using a language app to teach myself French, but the prompts were strange. Most of what I knew sounded like riddles. I couldn't ask "where is the metro station?" but I could state "the red horse eats bread" with real conviction. My first hour in Paris, I was too scared to leave the airport. I used the restroom and then sat in a booth at a coffee shop charging my phone until I amped myself up enough to take a shot at buying a metro ticket.

My debit card wouldn't read at the electronic ticket booth and a flustered man waiting in line behind me yelled something combatively at the back of my head and stomped off. The old woman smoking cigarettes behind him, sensing my distress, stepped forward and helped me make my purchase. After two hours of fumbling, I made it to the rental apartment where I would be staying. It was noon. I dropped my human-sized backpack in the middle of my room and it thudded against the wooden floorboards. My host, Céline, left a lovely welcome note on the desk. My mouth was dry and sour from the nine-hour flight.

The bathroom was narrow, fit for one human body. After showering, I accidentally locked myself in. I jiggled the handle and could feel myself beginning to panic. I stopped, conjured calmness, gently pulled the door toward me, and twisted. It opened. I breathed. I hobbled to the bedroom and dropped forward onto a mattress resting practically on the floor. I fell asleep immediately.

I stayed close to the apartment that night, grabbing dinner at a nearby restaurant, and then a pack of cigarettes at a bodega on the way home. I smoked the cigarettes on the bedroom balcony in the dark watching traffic, the moon, and a woman wearing an apron over her pajamas in the apartment across from me. She slashed a paintbrush across a paper canvas that she'd fixed to her living room wall.

When I woke up the next day, I dressed and then dreamily wandered the streets, misreading signs and informational boards. Each time I tried to use meager bits of the French I'd learned, people replied to me in English, as if my attempts were offensive (which they most likely were). *How will I ever perfect the language,* I wondered, *if no one allows me to speak it*? The city expressed a harmonious unification of form and function that dazzled me, a thing I didn't know a city could do. I was enchanted by the pastel color palette of the buildings, the elegant parks, and the flourish of architectural embellishments.

On my third day, I visited the National Museum of Natural History. I handed the woman behind a desk twelve glittering euros and she waved me forward toward the main room. The entrants were swallowed by brightness, baptized in natural light. Platforms with assembled bones stretched far and long toward a distant wall. All around me were kinetic children, buzzing like electrons, and parents wheeled empty strollers looking upward and awed. I was awed too.

I approached cautiously, and paused before a single North American mammoth femur that was taller than me. When no one was looking, I touched it. I *had* to. Its calcified surface was cold and smooth. I left my hand poised there while reading the small plaque at its base. "Kentucky" was scrawled in fine, French print. *Two American Southerners abroad* I thought. *Small world for me and the mammoth.*

I had never felt sad necessarily in considering the dinosaurs, but that day, standing beside their ossified remains, admiring the massive, thundering relics, I felt a little melancholy mixed with respect. *They're gone,* I thought. *Like* re ally *gone. They're never coming back.* I think I missed them or something. Big, magnificent, sentient beasts, I ogled their rib cages, imagining the weight of their skin. I pictured the thick layers of meat and muscle that used to cling to their heaving, breathing bones. I imagined the narratives each life possessed—the mammoth's mothers, brothers, and lovers.

Their skeletons were the ultimate totems of change. Peering up at the mammoth cinched by wires to the ceiling, I thought of Allie, gone from the earth. I considered all of us beasts scrambling to survive, doing our best, and how the sun burns overhead indifferently. It was sad, but was it actually? Or was it just the truth? It just *was. Our great end is timeless.*

• • •

Lying in bed with the lights off, I squinted at my cellphone in the dark. I had one full day left in Paris that was already stacked with activities, but something nagged at me to see an opera, even though I'd never seen an opera before. A strange craving. I knew downtown was the renowned Parisian opera house, the Palais Garnier. I'd passed it earlier in the day. I searched their website, there were no tickets for operas that month. There were, however, contemporary dances. I squirmed around on the mattress on the floor, reaching over the edge for my purse. I had far exceeded my budget, but this seemed important.

The following evening, I was running late. I lost track of time getting ready, while applying eyeshadow and sipping from a bottle of rosé. I called a taxi and carefully made my way toward the lobby, grasping the almost-vertical railing as I descended from the fifth-floor apartment. My feet wobbled in three-inch patent leather high heels.

The taxi that collected me was a BMW. I climbed in feeling dignified as we whirled over exquisite bridges toward downtown. I don't know why, probably because I was drunk, but I mistook the front of the building for the back, and I ran around the entire circumference of the place in my high heels before realizing. I entered the foyer, panting, and the steward scanned my ticket and motioned me inward. The foyer was empty and a man wearing a formal black vest immediately intercepted me.

He spouted off in French and I waited for him to finish. Through a shameful, pained expression I said, "I'm so sorry, I speak English."

"Okay," he said, "you are late. We can no longer let you into the theater to your ticketed seat because the show has begun. Let me see what we can do."

He passed me off to a sharp looking woman, also in all black, who spoke quickly. "We keep an extra seat open for situations like this."

I am a situation.

It was an unusual feeling to have my tardiness, and therefore sloppiness, accounted for ahead of time by strangers. Admittedly, I appreciated and admired the efficiency and acuity.

She pulled open a heavy door, put a finger to her lips, and led me through a short passageway with low, vaulted ceilings, carpeted in red velvet. Into the theater, she directed me up a brief set of steps and pointed to a metal folding chair, which I occupied hastily. I stuffed my purse and programs underneath.

The first act was unequivocally abstract. I strained to decode what exactly was happening, my guesswork fueled by the rosé. There were only three props on stage: stepping stones, a waist high tree made of twisted metal prongs, and a small altar. Four dancers stepped, crawled, and leapt curiously around stage. *Are they gods?* I theorized. *Are they metaphors for seasons? Are they in love? Is the one in the back a mother and the other three her children?* I opened the program and squinted at the words in the darkness.

Later on, I did my research and discovered I'd been watching the Martha Graham Dance company, which is the oldest American dance company, critically acclaimed, and named "one of the seven wonders of the artistic universe" by the *Washington Post.*[44] At the moment though, I consumed it like an uncultured swine.

What exactly am I seeing? Is this Cave of the Heart? *Or* Ekstasis? There were no descriptions. Flushed and swaying, I tried to make peace that I would never know why the woman dressed as the snake writhed at the base of the metal tree.

---

44 Alan M. Kriegsman, "Dance," *Washington Post,* March 29, 1989

At intermission I downed a glass of champagne.

The last dance in the sequence of performances was the longest at thirty full minutes. A series of women, arms interlocked, traipsed across the stage. Tall, hooded figures in black robes surrounded them. They selected one woman from the group, leading her away from the others by her wrist. The ballerina danced with a robed figure, even skipped with him, but as the dance continued a hierarchy clarified. The hooded figure watched from a pedestal above as the ballerina danced faster and more erratically. She spun from one side of the stage to the other, did arabesques, exhaustively darted, pirouetted, and glided. The hooded figure bound her by ropes and lifted her overhead.

Like a Rorschach test, I projected myself on her. I saw myself in her Herculean leaps. Pirouetting and dipping around the influences of my successive traumas. I saw how hastily they caused me to move around my life. Watching her, watching *myself*, I too felt exhausted. A victim of circumstance, fellow ballerinas circled the stage, observing her at a distance, and I wondered why they didn't come to her rescue. Angrily I asked, *Why won't anybody save her?*

I've thought about this play many times and I consider it differently now. I see myself as the hooded figure too. For me, they are one in the same.

In all the times I remember staying in abusive relationships, competing unnecessarily, violating my moral code, keeping quiet when needing to speak, or rushing into things, I see myself in the dark robes twirling, binding, and spinning *myself*. I no longer ask *when will someone rescue her?* I ask *when will she rescue herself?*

• • •

On the seventh day, I boarded a plane to Portugal with a box of macarons crushed into my backpack. In Lisbon, my taxi driver took me as close to my address as he could. He dropped me at the base of a steep hill. "I'm not allowed to drive through there. The streets are too narrow." I wandered the streets aimlessly on foot looking for my next dwelling. The host had sent his brother to collect me, who spoke no English. He stood before the front door, eyeing passersby skeptically.

He let me in and handed me an enormous metal key that corresponded to the front door lock. He left, closing the door behind him, I slouched against it, and closed my eyes. When I was ready to move again, I stepped toward windows at the far wall and pushed them open. A bouquet of houses with orange and red shingles spilled down a hillside toward the ocean. Laundry lines strung from one window to another. Pink and purple flowers boasted on patios and the fragrance of seafood wafted in.

I decided for the rest of my vacation I would reject social media. I wanted to make sure I was as present as possible for all the gifts my explorations might bring. I deleted the apps and tossed my cellphone on the bed. The universe answered my request.

With a few hours to spare before my dinner reservations, I opted to go on an introductory stroll. I stepped into the hall, twisted the key into the lock, and heard someone descending the stairs from the landing above mine—an elderly woman in her eighties with enormous baubles around her neck and loud, dangling earrings. I smiled at her as she came into view. She wobbled over uninhibited and gripped me by the elbow.

"Are we coming or going?"

"Going," I said.

"Well. Let's go, then!"

She pulled me forward and we exited the building together. Her head bobbed up and down with each quickened step over cobblestones. The alley she led me down spanned only ten feet wide. Doors to shops were thrown open, inviting visitors inward. Decorative, fabric flags arched over us. Men in sullied jeans and women in slouching tank tops leaned against doorways, arguing and smoking cigarettes.

She chattered hurriedly, explaining that the neighborhood, Alfama, was the oldest in the city, established in the year 1101 BC. "Most people were born here and have never left. They know nothing else beyond these walls. It is very important," she said "to remain respectful of the people and the architecture in order to preserve it." I nodded.

"This neighborhood has some of the best food in the world. The entire *world*. Do you hear me? *Especially* seafood. During your stay you must hear Fado music. Do you know it?"

On hearing I was visiting Lisbon, a friend of mine had suggested a restaurant. I didn't know anything about it, but I'd made a reservation in good faith. "I don't know what Fado is, but I made a dinner reservation at Clube de Fado," I said. "Is it good?"

She paused, touched a wrinkled hand to chest, and tossed her head back "only the best!"

We reached the end of the alley, which forked in two directions. "Where were you headed when I took you?" she asked.

"I was going to see the castle at the top of the hill." I pointed to a wide, easily paved road that slanted upward to our right. "Isn't this the way?"

"Yes," she said. "And that's why you're going this way. The longer way." She pulled her arm from mine, pressed her fingers into my back and pushed. I stumbled forward. "Get lost!" she shouted. I turned to watch her disappear through a cobalt door mounted in the alley wall.

Dazed, I floated down corridors, feeling lost, feeling scared, feeling excited. I was possessed by curiosity. Eyeballs from doorways scanned my naked thighs. The path wound upward and, positioned in the shade, an old man sold a vat of something from behind a cart with who I assumed to be his grandson at his side. I stepped up to the table. The child pushed a paper cup filled with coins forward. "How much?" I asked. The old man grinned and shrugged. The child pointed to a cardboard scrap with "€1" scrawled in marker. I slid a coin forward on the tabletop and the old man poured me a plastic cup of red liquid.

It was hooch—sweet, but stung my tongue. Turning echoing corners, I sipped from my cup, dipped through archways, climbing higher and higher, breaching the sun's rays. I felt spiritually elated, sailing above the collective unconscious in a beatified ambience of bliss. The exterior walls of each building wrapped in glittering tiles, like a kitchen backsplash, as if Portuguese houses were pulled inside out. On every street corner a dignified portrait of a man or a woman from history was mounted into the wall. I liked this. There was something romantic about the figures of Portuguese history aging with the architecture they ruled.

Overlooking the sloping city, a feeling moved through me—something that I had felt only with people, but never a place. I was *in love.* It was amorousness. Music from somewhere softly infused the air. A few feet ahead, a man stood against a chain-link fence with an open suitcase at his feet. He looked to be my age, tall, tan skinned, with dreadlocks pulled into a band above his head. His eyes were easy and kind. His art was clipped to the fence beside him and he watched while I examined each piece—collages composed of *National Geographic* magazine scraps.

I pointed to a portrait of a woman who I found particularly appealing. The bust was composed of earth tone textures and the head made up of what looked like the petals of a white poinsettia. She was striking.

"How much for this one?" I asked sweetly.

"It's actually a series of three," he said. "This is the first image of a woman becoming her truest self."

I pulled out my wallet. "I'll take them all."

• • •

At 7:00 p.m., I relaxed against a table in the hall of Clube de Fado fanning myself with a brochure. My attention turned to the doorway when a wide, stout woman plunged through it gasping. She gripped the doorframe and heaved herself in. I noticed her silver hair first, shaved on one side. Very chic. She caught her breath and moved toward me to fan herself with a brochure too. I heard her mutter something to the maitre d'. Her accent was British.

After seven days of talking mostly to myself, I was relieved to hear my own language. As we waited to be allowed into the dining room, I started a conversation. Her name was Helena. I was surprised to hear Helena say in her butterscotch accent that she was all the way from the West Coast of America. The host approached and asked if he could seat us together at the same table to conserve space. Helena and I exchanged an awkward glance. We agreed.

Something about Helena seemed worldly, and across from her I felt childish and juvenile. I guessed she was in her sixties.

She scanned me carefully. "What'll you be having to drink?" I could tell the question was charged.

"The house wine," I said nervously, as if I was being tested.

"Which one?"

"Red. Merlot?"

She looked pleased.

The waiter took our drink order and she copied me. *Huh.* She ordered the octopus. I ordered the steak. After two glasses of wine, the gaits of our personalities changed color.

"Where are you from?" she asked. Her eyes flicked to the tattoo on my forearm.

"Florida," I said. A glimmer of insecurity.

"Ha!" she chortled. "I wouldn't have guessed that."

A smirk quivered on my lips.

"You seem educated. You present yourself well." Offense and flattery tethered into one.

Helena was a physicist and a sommelier. "I always order the house wine," she said, "because it will tell me everything I need to know about a place." She was born in Pakistan. As a teenager, she renounced her religion and fled to England where she attended college, then adopted Christianity. When she mentioned Christianity, it was the only time through our conversation that I spied a glimmer of bashfulness in her. She moved from England to New York City, and lived on the Upper East side for fifteen years before moving to California, where she's lived ever since.

During the equivalent of two bottles of wine, we covered a wide range of topics.

"So you work for *National Geographic,* but are you happy?" She asked, slanting over a half-chewed octopus.

"Hm. I don't know. Some days I am and some days I'm not. Some days I think I know what I want and the next day I think I want something else. I have a hard time understanding what is realistic around the word 'happy.'"

"In physics," she started "there is a theory of infinitude. Think of time as infinity. I need you to think for yourself, now. If you had infinite time on the earth to do whatever you wanted, are you doing that right now?"

I paused. "No."

"Then you need to make a change."

I told her I'd been considering going back to school, but I was a bit embarrassed for my age. She held out her empty glass as the waiter poured another serving of wine.

"When I was thirty-two," she said, "I saw an academic advisor about getting my PhD. He asked me 'Helena, do you know how old you'll be when you graduate? Thirty-six.' I told him 'I'd rather be thirty-six with my PhD than without it.'"

I liked Helena.

"Why are you here?" She asked. "Why are you traveling all alone?"

"I could ask you the same question," I joked.

"I'm grieving." She frowned. "I lost my poor Bella. I booked this vacation to lift my spirits."

I waited for her to reveal the name and shape of such a creature.

"Bella was my precious Corgi. She owned my house, had an entire room to herself. She pranced around with the air of a dignitary! I was absolutely *heartbroken* when she died. No one and nothing will ever replace her. So," she said, forking more octopus into her mouth, "now *you* tell *me*. Why are you here?"

I was beleaguered by the question. Not because I was troubled by speaking about Allie's death, which was something factual to me, like reporting the weather. But because I'd learned that revealing the death of a loved one contains two parts to a script. The first part is the revealing of it, which sounds like "my sister died." The second part is the emotional labor of restoring comfort to the conversation, as the inquirer inevitably becomes uncomfortable by my reply. When they say "I'm so sorry," while looking uncomfortable, I say "thank you." Because 'thank you' is the only reply that keeps newly grieving people appearing sane. Or "it's okay," even though it never will be.

"I'm traveling alone because I'm grieving the death of my sister. She died one year ago, this week."

Helena's face fell. "I am *so* sorry. Here I am talking about my dog, and your poor sister."

"Don't be sorry. I am so sorry for your Bella."

A hesitation rippled between us.

"How did it happen? Was she ill?"

"Motorcycle accident."

Helena looked sullen.

"Isn't it a little odd though that grief brought us both here together in the same night?"

"Odd indeed," she said.

The Fado performance began—a special Portuguese singing accompanied by a classical Portuguese guitar. We halted our conversation, tilted inward with rosy cheeks, and watched a beautiful woman across the room bellow notes with a verve sourced from deep inside her guts. Her hand rested on the shoulder of a beefy man seated on a wooden chair at her hip. He played a stringed instrument that looked much like an acoustic guitar, but different. After each song, I noticed she squeezed his shoulder affectionately. That was my favorite part, their little secret.

A film formed over Helena's eyes. The performers took a break and we reclined in our seats and looked around. "I told you," she said. "This music makes you horny. You should only attend Fado if you have someone to go home with." Our eyes moved to the busser hunched at the table beside us. I watched her face as she studied him. She looked at me, then at him, and back at me. "The music wasn't *that* good." We almost spit out our wine we laughed so hard.

"When was your last lover?" She asked.

"Eight months ago. But it's complicated. It took a year to move toward commitment and then it was destroyed in a single day."

She folded her arms across her chest, thinking of something. "Well, life is long. You will probably see him again. You will be *shocked* at who reenters your life." She shot me an intense look. "They *always* come back." In a sudden wash of serenity, she asked "And no one currently?"

"No. I've been taking a break from dating. In fact, now that I'm starting to feel secure, I think I'm afraid to fall in love again."

She drained a little more of her glass and shook her head from side to side. "Honey, no no no. You *cannot* be afraid. You also learn who you are through loving and losing. Fall in love as many times as you can, and as soon as you can."

20

RHETORIC

I took Helena's words to heart. In October 2018, after seven months of singlehood, I told myself *I'm ready.* I wanted to try dating again. And date I did. However, after my fifth bad date in three weeks with various gentlemen I met on dating apps, I sat at my desk with my head in my hands, crying. My phone glowed on the table in front of me, faces of strangers ready for the swiping on screen. *Why not me?*

Shrouded in the enchantment of fall, everyone around me was falling in love: my friends, my ex-boyfriends, my coworkers. Even my landlord had a new beau who joined her for afternoon cocktails on the porch. I could hear them laughing from my unit downstairs.

Why not me?

I'd made a list of the type of person I wanted, and I had stuck to it. I'd not kissed or slept with any of my dates. I'd made cuts right away, weeding out the ones who didn't measure up. I'd made myself available, joined all the clubs, dating apps and sites. I thought if I checked all the traditional boxes on the recipe list for companionship, *poof,* my radical, earth shattering union should appear.

Why not me?

I had only made myself available for twenty-one days, but I thought I could call on love like fast-food delivery. That I could go online and book my perfect mate at my leisure like a plane ticket. I swiped through potential suitors with the same nonchalance as I did while online shopping, anticipating love with expedited shipping.

Why not me?

In a way, my disappointment was justified. I deserved love and to be loved exactly as I was, without having to suffer first, or become a perfect person, as patriarchal narratives might have one believe. However, I disregarded a crucial aspect of the companionship recipe: time. Instead, I assumed the massive responsibility of the universe by trying to force exactly when a compatible partner might tumble into my life. I thought I could overrule the magic of chance and the virtue of patience by throwing a temper tantrum.

Why not me?

It is much easier to be alone while actively rejecting romantic companionship than it is to be alone while wanting it. The latter requires hope and surrender. My impatience muddied this period of discomfort and I couldn't see it as teaching me something valuable. Something like: even when we *think* we are ready, the universe has to agree. Something like: enjoy living a worthy life in the interim, *regardless* of what happens.

The morning after my fifth bad date, I deleted all of my dating apps. I logged out of the online sites too. My devices were purged. I left my phone at home and went for a walk through my neighborhood in the early morning light. *Fine, universe* I thought as I admired lavender overgrowing a plot planted in sidewalk. *I'm ready for a mind blowing, eternal partnership* right now, *but if you want me to wait, I will wait.*

That's when the universe tested me.

Spoiler alert: I failed the test. Turns out, I was not willing to wait because that night I invited someone home from a bar with me.

The test wasn't about sex, as much as it was about whether or not I would listen to my intuition. Whether or not I would keep holding out for a good fit. But sex flushed my mind with hormones and clouded my judgment. Sex made it difficult to determine whether or not we were compatible.

Surprisingly, the one-night stand did turn into a relationship. But I was too clouded to leave it when it turned sour. The red flags could've been baked neatly into a key-lime pie, smashed into my face, and I still would've bypassed them. The vow I had made after Allie died—to shut down pain portals—slowly eroded through our increased arguing. At first, we argued once a month, then weekly, and then every other day. But I was *ready* to date and I wanted to *prove* it, which, ironically, proved the exact opposite.

As I floundered to control the escalating stress our incompatibility brought, I lost my handle on everything else. Specifically, my finances. I had fallen back into credit card debt and was desperately trying to claw my way out.

Nine months in, our second-to-last blowout, the runner up fight of all fights, was over (wait for it!) a cannoli.

I had just come home from an interview for a part-time job, in addition to my full-time job, at a bakery.

"How'd it go?" my partner asked flatly from the couch, scrolling on his phone. My superpowers prickled.

"Good!" I chirped, setting my things on the kitchen counter. "The place is really cute inside. If they hire me, I'll probably pick up two or three shifts a week. Mostly on the weekends."

"Hmph."

"We had coffee during the interview and I think the manager liked me. I ordered some of the treats to try. The cannoli were *amazing*."

Without looking up, he said "cannoli suck."

"...what?"

He tipped his head up from the phone and looked me squarely in the eye, "Cannoli. They're disgusting."

"I mean, I like them. I think they're pretty good."

"Nah. All Italian pastries suck, actually. They're nasty."

I didn't understand what was happening. I could feel my stress response activating. *Was that a dig at me? At my heritage?* I suspected his gruffness wasn't actually about the cannoli at all, but I muzzled my intuition. *It's just a cannoli,* I told myself. *Why am I getting so defensive? Maybe he's just joking.* I tried to participate in the joke by pushing back.

"Oh yeah? Well I think Bulgarian desserts are gross. Who wants shriveled dates and prunes in their dessert? Ew."

Wrong move. The argument intensified at warp speed. Fifteen minutes later I was sobbing on the floor. He stood in the doorframe, laughing and ridiculing. The sadder I was, the angrier he became, which made me even more sad, and so on and so forth. He accused me of being overly emotional. I accused him of having anger issues. We broke up a month later. The bakery never called me back.

It was over, but ten months of nonstop fighting had left me emotionally, financially, and energetically ravaged. Lying on top of my made bed in the middle of the day, I asked *After everything I have been through, how did I get here again? Why do my relationships always end in theatric combustions? Why do I repeatedly end up depleted?*

These were not rhetorical questions.

To recover and to find the answers I knew I might need a substantial amount of time to myself. Even though I was in no position to jump into a relationship anyway, I vowed to quit dating for a full year. Although, a year sounded like an eternity. I decided to break it into small pieces, to check in with myself every three months and reevaluate things. I'd fill the time and space with an internal investigation.

Quitting was contagious. It spread across the borders of my life, from the relationship sector to everywhere else. With no one to woo, I suddenly quit straightening my hair. I recognized the habit for what it was: a tactic that aided me in seeking belonging outside of myself. I didn't even know what my natural hair looked like anymore. I unplugged the hair straightener from the wall, wrapped the cord around the handles, zipped it into a backpack, and zipped that backpack into a suitcase that I thrust out of sight into the depths of my closet.

I quit emotional spending. I realized my finances were only going to get better if I stopped any unnecessary purchases immediately—until I could hold boundaries with myself and I could understand my beliefs around money. I sealed my credit card in a Tupperware dish full of water and inserted the Tupperware into the freezer.

I quit putting myself in positions that made me feel bad, compromised, or unsafe. On a Friday night, all of my friends dressed up to head across town to a swanky party I knew my ex would be attending. I really wanted to go, to dress up in a too tight garment, an abundance of cleavage. Instead I put on my sweatpants and wrestled my Swiffer out of the utility closet. For four hours straight, I Swiffered, and wiped, and vacuumed until it was 1:00 a.m. and I knew the party would be over—I was safe from temptation.

I quit investing my energy in anything that wasn't providing an equal return.

• • •

To pay off my debts, I sought out more part-time jobs. I got one as a farmer's market cashier, a dog walker, and in October of 2019 I was hired by a local coffee shop as a wedding caterer on nights and weekends. The extra income was a relief but would require social sacrifices. I was scared to miss out on things. I imagined having no friends and becoming forgotten. But I didn't really have another option. I was forced into trust. *It's going to be okay* I told myself. *There will always be other social events. This year isn't about anyone else, but me. The right people will be there for me on the other side of this.*

"No, I can't go roller-skating on Saturday at the outdoor disco. I'm working."

"No, I can't grab drinks on the rooftop at dusk. I'm working."

"No, I'll need to miss the group picnic in the park. I'm working."

"No, I can't make it to your Halloween party. I'm working."

After my first full day of catering training, I walked through the coffee shop patio gate, rounded the corner, and climbed into my car parked on the street. I unfolded a paper with my schedule printed on it. Dread washed over me. I reached for my phone to text my friend Gemma. I typed out the message, my fingers weakening by the letter. "No, it looks like I can't go to Philly for your birthday anymore. I'm so sorry. I'm working." *She'll be okay with it, right? She should understand. She knows I'm drowning in debt. I only have $300 in my savings account, and I have to pay rent next week. Spending three days eating out and partying in Philly would be ludicrous for my circumstances. She'll support me.*

Wrong. She was hurt.

One after another, crying emojis sailed into my inbox. The more she detailed how hurt she was, how she felt like I didn't care about her, the more I postured and counterbalanced with justifications. Back and forth we texted: at work, on the bus, eating lunch, after yoga, in our beds. Like with Daniel, I was incapable of fielding her disappointment. I apologized politely, and said I would try to make it up, but when I read her texts, instead of feeling compassion, I felt anger.

On the third day of arguing I went frigid. Heading home from the grocery store, at a stop sign I wrote "I'm exhausted. I'm sorry, but I can't discuss this any longer." I threw my phone agitatedly into my purse and drove the rest of the way in silence. When I parked, I rolled my shoulders back. They felt stiff, and so did my chest. I pulled the paper grocery bags from the trunk, lugged them inside, and dropped them on the kitchen table. I tossed my keys in the bowl and laid down on the couch.

What is wrong with me? My whole body was rigid. My jaw clenched and so did my hands. I picked at an oval stain in the couch fabric from spilled nail polish remover with my fingernail. Then it hit me like a sack of cannoli. *I'm back in my old relationship.* Except it was a role reversal. My best friend was me (sad) and I was my ex (angry).

While I didn't amplify my anger to ridicule, like my ex had done, I had judged her as being overly emotional, and not caring about my needs. Her reaction caused me to feel that I wasn't just *doing* bad by cancelling our plans, but that I *was* bad.

There is a critical difference between "doing" bad and "being" bad.[45] One is guilt and one is shame. Guilt self-talk

45 Brené Brown, *Daring Greatly: How the Courage to Be Vulnerable Transforms the Way We Live, Love, Parent, and Lead* (New York: Avery, 2015), 71.

sounds like "I can't believe I *did* that. What a crappy thing to do." Shame self-talk sounds like "I'm such an idiot. I'm a terrible friend."[46] While guilt causes psychological discomfort that can help us to do better, shame corrodes the part of us that believes we can do better.[47]

My entire life I had condemned the emotion of anger. Anyone expressing it toward me was perceived as cruel or barbaric. Yet, I attracted it. Coursing through my lineage, I felt uniquely haunted. Echoes on the theme presented in boyfriends, coworkers, or bosses. I alienated myself from my own anger too. I couldn't bear the idea that I had the ability to hurt people like I had been hurt. Anger never touched me, or so I believed.

But of course I had anger. I rolled over on my side, closed my eyes and visions of anger bouts came into focus:

The time that Jarred pulled me aside during the middle of a concert by my favorite musician. In the center of a roaring crowd, he shouted "I need to tell you something." Then expressed he didn't want to move in with me. *Ever.* We left the concert early and went back to his house, where I blew up. "I'm not angry!" I yelled, lifting my bicycle over my head and hurling it from the top step of his porch into the street. It crashed below, clattering like the symbols on a drum set.

The time my most recent ex had denied me sex. Feeling confused and rejected, I flew into a fury, even stomped my feet like a child. I slammed the door as I exited the apartment.

The time in the post office when I'd asked the clerk behind the counter to give me a price quote for shipping a

46 Ibid.

47 Brené Brown, *Daring Greatly: How the Courage to Be Vulnerable Transforms the Way We Live, Love, Parent, and Lead* (New York: Avery, 2015), 72.

painting. "I need to send this painting across the country soon," I said, "but could you weigh it and tell me how much the shipping would be? It's still a bit wet. If you can just place it on the scale, touching only the edges that are dry, I'd appreciate it." The clerk accepted the painting, immediately stuck his finger into its wet center, and looked at me horrified. "It's wet!" he claimed, angrily. "I know!" I spat. "Jesus, I just told you that!" I rolled my eyes, huffed and puffed, and snatched the painting from his grip as he wiped oil paint off his thumb with a tissue. Customers stared as I tore out of the lobby.

Anger is like a deep-fried, tube-shaped cannoli shell. It is thin, flaky, and hollow on the outside, shielding a dense filling of *fear* and *shame* on the inside, usually spilling out from either end.

Made aware of the pain I caused, I couldn't feel sympathy for Gemma because, underneath my anger, I was fearful of being ostracized or unlovable. However, participating in the altercation through the eyes of anger, I was able to understand anger from the inside out. And I was fascinated. I wanted to understand everything about anger—an emotion that had set a tone for my life. I purchased books on anger, nonviolent communication, and conflict resolution, hoping to become a rubber stopper on the electrical wire of anger and shame. To diffuse the current from flowing beyond me.

When I examined the dynamic between anger and shame objectively, like poking around a diorama, anger wasn't so scary any more. I realized the emotion wasn't wrong; it was even healthy and warranted in some cases. I was able to look back on my life with more compassion for myself when I had expressed anger, but also for others when they had expressed anger with me. The more I identified and claimed my anger, the more I understood *accountability.* Accountability relocated me from victimized to empowered.

• • •

Gemma and I made up. A few weeks later, in November of 2019, she texted me a link. "I really think you should try this!" she wrote. I saw the text while clocking out of my morning shift at the farmer's market. When I got home, I planted myself in a chair on my porch and removed my sneakers. I smelled like sweat and my muscles throbbed from lifting crates of vegetables. I picked up my phone and clicked the link in my inbox. It guided me to a series of classes led by a group named To Be Magnetic (TBM). I massaged my thigh with my free hand as I scrolled the website. Birds chirped. The teachings seemed to ascribe to a philosophy of healing childhood wounds, which dictate the functionality of our adult lives.[48] *Hm. Interesting.* A subscription to the content was eighteen dollars a month. I was skeptical.

I revisited the link several times over the weeks, my curiosity unshakeable, but I worried the lessons would be too superstitious for my liking. That I would end up getting swindled. I chatted with a friend about it over a Saturday morning jog. "Pffft. Sounds like pseudoscience," she said. But in December of 2019 my curiosity overtook me. There was a free guided meditation on the website called Clarity.[49] I gave it a go.

Before bed, I pulled my eye mask over my eyes, popped in my ear buds, and hit the play button. Thirty minutes later, I uncovered my eyes, and wiped away hot tears. What I had seen

---

48 "Neural Manifestation™," To Be Magnetic, accessed March 26, 2021.

49 "Free Exercise: Get Clarity," To Be Magnetic, accessed March 18, 2021.

was not superstition, but the magic of possibility. My unconscious desires rising to the surface, I'd envisioned myself as a forty-year-old woman, balancing a toddler on my hip and making coffee. I kissed my husband before heading out the door to open my shop for the day in downtown Portland, Maine. I'd envisioned myself writing stories from a small, quiet room, gazing out a window that showed the hugeness of the desert. I'd envisioned myself as an old woman, sitting contentedly at a picnic table in the backyard of my mountain home, string lights winking, hosting a family gathering.

My unconscious showed me what I might like for my future self, if my path was no longer dictated by trauma or chaos and if I made choices from a place of desire, joy, and worth, rather than survival.

• • •

In mid-March of 2020, six months into my self-audit, the global Covid 19 pandemic struck. With the rest of the nation, my coworkers and I were sent home to quarantine for the unforeseeable future. Leadership estimated it'd only last for "a few weeks." Those weeks turned into a month, then months. Though rattled and fearful, I considered myself lucky to have my job, my health, and a stable environment to quarantine.

Coincidentally, the outward, global upheaval mirrored my inward, personal upheaval. Reaching the halfway point of my single year, I checked in with myself about dating. To my surprise, I was enjoying being alone and focusing on myself. The interior of my apartment, a one-bedroom basement unit of a row-house, transformed into a cocoon.

In the months I was sequestered indoors, I became a miner of myself. I had purchased a subscription to TBM, which was helping me look inward. Truth seeking was my duty and unconscious beliefs formed in childhood were my treasure. Clocking out of my day job, I reported to the night shift at my couch in uniform (pink striped pajamas) with my chisel (pen) and pan (journal). In my excavations, other denied aspects of myself rippled to the surface.[50] Like with anger, I found that I feared being selfish, stupid, fat, ugly, a bitch, and unlovable. These words made me uncomfortable and embarrassed to jot down.

Each word was a concept that had a beginning in my history; a time when I'd internalized selfishness, stupidity, fatness, ugliness, bitchiness, and unlovability as being "wrong" versus "right." I noticed that all of my concepts ultimately tethered back to "unlovability," the ultimate non-belonging, and I wanted to explore that more. Using the tools I picked up from TBM, in the darkness of the mine, which was actually my couch, I closed my eyes.[51]

Whoosh! It was 2001 on the screen of my mind. My twelve-year-old body stood in the doorway of my mother's bedroom. Pink carpet threaded between my toes. Mom was on the floor sobbing. I watched her, saying nothing. I was unsympathetic and aggravated. She looked up from the floor, wiped her eyes, and said, "You know, I wish I never had children. It's very unfulfilling." Pain radiated through me. *Unlovable.* I watched my feet through my twelve-year-old eyes race across the house and into my bedroom. I closed the door behind me.

My mind screen went black.

Whoosh! The scene reset. I was back in the doorway and Mom was back on the carpet. However, this time there

---

50 "Learn the Lingo: Manifestation Glossary," To Be Magnetic, accessed March 18, 2021.

51 "Neural Manifestation TM," To Be Magnetic, accessed March 18, 2021.

were three of us. My thirty-year-old self was standing in the doorway beside my twelve-year-old self. I observed the situation through my adult eyes. My mother looked up from the floor, wiped her tears, and said the unlovable thing. "Having children is very unfulfilling." On cue, my twelve-year-old self ran into her bedroom and closed the door.

This time, my older self walked calmly down the hall, into my bedroom, and held the younger me. I rubbed my own little back, hugged myself tightly, and said "it's okay, Nicki. Sometimes adults get stressed, and this makes them say hurtful or untrue things. What she said isn't true. You are a gift, and you deserve to be here just like everybody else. You are very, very loved."

I removed my twelve-year-old self from the house by taking her on a drive to Dairy Queen. We ate M&M ice creams with red plastic spoons, while listening to NSYNC and wiggling in our seats. When back at the house, I sent my twelve-year-old self to her bedroom and peeled off to confront my forty-five-year-old mom.

When I saw the anguish in Mom's face, as my thirty-year-old self, I understood the situation from an aerial perspective. She was working, going to night school, and managing Allie's behavior. I saw that she sorely needed a break from the relentlessness of life. I understood that what she had said to me that night, as personal as it felt, wasn't about me at all. Still, I gave myself the voice I needed back then.

"Mom," said my dream self, "I know you're stressed while working hard to support this family. I'm *so* sorry that things are so hard right now. But you can't say things like that to a kid. Even if I'm being a brat. I don't know any better than to internalize that messaging. I'll imbue the belief that I'm unlovable all the way into my late twenties. You need to calm down and go apologize to me for saying that."

Whoosh! I zoomed back to the present.

My mining work was deep, private, emotional reparation. My goal wasn't to stir up old drama or implant false memories. My goal was to *let go.* At times I reached out to people from my past, in the present, to hear more about their sides of the stories I wanted to address. This was helpful, but oftentimes, like with my mom, so much time had passed since the incidents occurred, they were no longer the same person as they were back then. Thus, revisiting the wounds in my mind gave me the directness to mend them at the source. My wiser self, in all I had learned through my life, gave my younger self the love, healing, and closure to move on.

• • •

Instead of continuing to deny my selfishness, stupidity, fatness, ugliness, bitchiness, and unlovability, I embraced it. The truth was, at various points in my life, I had been all of these things. If I tried hard enough, I could unearth proof of me being *all sorts* of things—sometimes even two antonyms at once, like a victim and a victimizer. I had been cheap, fraudulent, mean, and lazy. But I also found proof of myself being generous, genuine, kind, and industrious. I discovered these words across my life map not because I am ultra-unique, but because *every person is all of these things.* Each person houses the whole of the human spectrum.[52] While undoubtedly shaped by our environments, each human is 99.9 percent similar to the person beside them.[53] We are made up of and motivated by (mostly) the same stuff.

---

52 "Q/A Index Library: Unblocked Shadow," To Be Magnetic, accessed March 18, 2021.

53 Lydia Ramsey Pflanzer, Samantha Lee, "Our DNA Is 99.9% the Same as the Person Next to Us," Business Insider, accessed March 18, 2019.

Whenever I found myself judging someone else in a negative way, I got into the habit of asking *how am I like that too?* For example, while passing the quarantine days that blurred into one another, if I were watching reality television on my laptop, I saw lip fillers, teeth implants, nose jobs, and thought *Wow. These people are so fake!* Then I asked myself *Okay and what about me?* I considered my own physical modifications that could be considered as fake: makeup, hair dye, Instagram filters, shaving my body hair, push up bras, anti-aging creams, compression leggings, and so on.

When I reminded myself that everyone has the capacity to be everything, the fear and shame leaking out of my unconscious dissipated. I was more easily able to accept feedback in both my personal and working life because I felt less personally attacked, I wasn't mired by self-pity. I found balance in determining what was and wasn't mine to own. I grew into knowing I was inherently worthy of love and belonging no matter what words were held up against me.

"We are psychologically, emotionally, cognitively, and spiritually hard wired for connection, love, and belonging. Connection...is why we are here, and it is what gives purpose and meaning to our lives."[54] We don't have to accept, like, or agree with everything or everyone we encounter. However, in recognizing our mutual humanity, in taking accountability, we can empathize, forgive, and communicate more effectively.

---

54 Brené Brown, *Daring Greatly: How the Courage to Be Vulnerable Transforms the Way We Live, Love, Parent, and Lead* (New York: Avery, 2015), 68.

21

CHANGE

I pinched the rim of a ceramic dish in my left hand, in which was teetering an Oreo tower. I selected an Oreo from the top of the stack with my right hand, dipped it midway into a glass of milk on the coffee table, and set it on my tongue. I bit down hard on the cookie when I heard a thud from above.

A pause. Pitter pattering. Banging.

Something scampered back and forth in the ceiling overhead. It was late April of 2020. Having been isolated in my basement for almost two months, I knew I was getting a bit weird, but this wasn't a fabrication of my imagination. I set down the cookie dish and shifted cautiously into a standing position. *What could it be?*

Closets bookended both sides of the living room. One closet was walk-in size, containing a massive water heater. The other closet was small and shallow, containing a set of pipes. My eyes scoured the white plaster ceiling as the creature scuttled from one side of the house to the other.

Bang! The sound came from the closet with the water heater. *Oh no oh no oh no oh no oh no.* Much like the creature, I scampered around the living room in circles, helpless, heart and mind racing. *I've heard mice before and that is not a mouse.*

Too big, way too big. Could it be a raccoon? Oh God, what if it's a rat? The closet banging stopped. It was in the ceiling again. Bang! The sound came from the other closet. *Jesus,* I swore, *it's going to burst through the door and ravage me!*

I dialed a number I found on Google for pest control. The man on the line was rather relaxed, considering the beast I mentioned readying itself to barge through my walls. "It's probably a squirrel," he said. "This happens all the time."

"A squirrel? But how would it get into my ceiling?" I asked. "I'm all the way down in the basement unit."

"Sometimes they crawl through a hole in the roof and follow the pipes down into the rest of the house. It probably got turned around in there."

"How soon can you be here?" The thudding was getting louder.

"Two to three hours."

We hung up the phone and I rummaged through my art supplies until I found a roll of laughably flimsy painter's tape. I ran the tape around the frame of each closet door, sealing off any open spaces. I couldn't risk the unbearable possibility of glimpsing a tail or a talon sweeping through a crack. I leaned two kitchen chairs under each door knob too. At first glance, one might think I'd trapped a wild boar in there.

The three hours it took pest control to come were nerve-racking. I paced, and sighed, and wrung my hands. I tried to distract myself from the creature's distress sounds by going for a walk around the block. Except on the walk, all I could think about was coming home to find the closet doors thrown open, recklessly hanging from their hinges.

When pest control finally arrived, an enormous man, handsome, chiseled, dressed like a real-life G.I. Joe, knocked on the back door of the upstairs unit. My landlord let him in. In his hand was a net. The net was puny and looked silly against the importance of his outfit. "Where is it?" he asked stoically. I led him downstairs to the water heater closet and backed against the stairwell. He placed a hand on the closet doorknob and crouched into a defensive stance.

"You ready for this?" he asked, over his shoulder.

"Yes!" I squeaked, squinting one eye.

He twisted the knob and flung the door open. Nothing. Blackness. He stooped under the door frame and poked his head inside. The banging intensified. "It's coming from behind the drywall. I'm going to have to break through it. You have a hammer or anything?"

"Uh... There should be a pair of rollerblades in there somewhere."

He looked down, picked a rollerblade up off the floor, cocked it back, and bashed the wheels through the drywall, creating a broad hole. "Oh!" he exclaimed. I stepped forward and peeked into the closet, under his armpit. To both our surprise, out of the hole flapped the iridescent wings of a European Starling. Before he could grasp his net, the bird flew out of the closet, up the stairs, and out the back door.

The G.I. Joe smiled at me. Particles of drywall peppered his front. "Starlings are curious animals," he said, shrugging off the occurrence. I thanked him for coming and my landlord walked him out.

Like drywall dust suspended in the air, residue of the starling hung in my mind for weeks. I was bewildered by how something so rackety and clamorous, burrowed so deep, could fly free with such ease. While I'd interpreted its sounds as menacing, I mourned not opening the closet door sooner. The rhythm of its thudding for release was familiar, something I recognized from my internal world.

• • •

Ram Dass once said, "If you think you are enlightened, go and spend a week with your parents."[55]

The government set an expectation that quarantine would extend until August 2020, minimum. The stay-at-home orders presented contradictory circumstances. On one hand, with so much alone time for introspection, I was making remarkable progress in my self-healing work. On the other hand, by May I was nearing madness. My ceilings were low and my apartment was dark. I craved sunshine and open space. The strangest of my cravings was for extended in-person eye contact. The only eye contact I made with other humans happened during brief and stressful trips to the grocery store. Otherwise, it was through a screen.

In early May, I asked my mom if it would be okay if I came to Florida to stay with her, my stepdad, and my niece for the summer. She said yes, and the following week I made the fourteen-hour drive to my parent's house in Ormond Beach.

Not having straightened my hair for a full nine months, I looked different than any of the times they had seen me in the last sixteen years. As hair recovering from heat and chemical damage tends to get fuller before it gets longer, my head was an explosion of tendrils. Additionally, the curls prevented me from sliding my fingers through and breaking off brittle, split ends, which there were naturally less of. Formerly short and broken patches of hair at the nape of my neck, crown, and temples were flooded with soft, new, curly hairs. Coupled

---

55 Eckhart Tolle, *A New Earth: Awakening to Your Life's Purpose* (New York: Viking Press, 2005) 100.

with my nightly journaling that served as a release, the urge to pull had disappeared almost entirely.

This new version of myself set up my things in my childhood bedroom—the place I'd been revisiting in my mind's eye. The irony was not lost on me as I refilled the spaces I'd grown out of. I slept in my childhood bed under my childhood comforter and packed my toiletries into the bathroom cabinets wrought with scrunchies I'd used in 2003. My mom helped position a desk in my bedroom in front of a large window that I worked remotely from during the day. When I wasn't working, I drove a short distance to the sanctuary of the beach. I laid in the sun and floated in the waves. I went for long, aimless walks along the shore. At night, I crawled into Mom's bed with her and watched TV. Different, but the same.

On transition, American neuroscientist David Eagleman says, "Every moment of your life, your brain is rewiring. You've got eighty-six billion neurons and a fraction of a quadrillion connections between them. These vast seas of connections are constantly changing their strength, and they're unconnecting and reconnecting elsewhere. It's why you are a slightly different person than you were a week ago or a year ago."[56]

Visiting old environments has a way of highlighting transpired change. After nine months of singledom, paying off all of my credit card debt, wearing my hair curly, and burning through a slew of literature on finance, communication, meditation, adult attachment, and shame, I felt dramatic intellectual shifts. Implementing so many healthy, consistent habits at such a rapid clip rocked me. Indications

---

56 Steve Paulson, "Your Brain Makes You a Different Person Every Day," *Nautilus*, October 14, 2020.

of these brain shifts struck me in physical manifestations, while my mind was at rest, on a drive or walking beside the ocean. Momentary, mental lurches that felt like I was moving very slowly and very quickly all at once.

I was willing to give myself credit for these changes, to have the audacity to celebrate myself even in the tumult of the world at large. That was proof of my changing too.

• • •

At 3:00 a.m., smack dab in the middle of July, I finally woke up.

Like a meteoroid smashing through my bedroom window in the dead of night, I opened my eyes, launched forward, and waved a hand around in the dark, searching for the beaded string of the bedside Tiffany lamp. My fingers touched chain and I yanked down hard. Light exploded into the room. I stumbled out of bed, tripping over tangled sheets, and falling off the mattress. On my desk, I uncovered my journal beneath a pile of papers.

I'd just had a dream. The Foil: Aaron.

While I had barely spoken to Aaron in nine years, except for one or two rare messages, I was never fully able to get over him. Lovers passed through my life, but each time a relationship failed, whispers flushed the back of my mind: *What if? What if we* were *meant to be together all those years ago? What if he was right? What if I never find a love that's as electrifying and passionate in body and mind? What if I never meet anyone like* him*?*

Except we *were* still communicating, only indirectly. One of the malevolent functions of social media is that it can hinder one from moving on, by way of micro consumption. We nurse old attachments by taking sips of people through their social media activity. For nine years, I watched Aaron watch me. I wasn't following his social channels, but I noticed his daily likes, his impressions, and views on mine.

Every so often, I asked myself *what does all this micro attention mean? Why does he care what I'm up to? What does he think of me now? How long will this carry on for? Will we observe one other from afar until we die?* He was an open question I couldn't satisfy. I assumed the passage of time would ease my fixation, but every six months he made a cameo in my dreams. I wondered if something was seriously wrong with *me,* not with the toxic pressures of the technology or society.

But the dream on this night was not just a dream, it was a second sight. An awakening.

My pupils were still dilated and, squinting, I scribbled down my revelations into my journal so I would remember them in the morning. On my mind screen, while sleeping, my brain had relived our time together. I watched the playback of my sophomore year of college: Aaron and I listening to records in his dorm room, pouring over artists in my textbooks, and screening too cool, indie movies. However, there was an audio annotation over these scenes. The annotation pointed out the feelings of enchantment I experienced with him were a projection from my own beautiful mind. I was able to identify the beauty in the aforementioned art forms because I carry that same beauty within *myself.*

I had incorrectly associated those feelings with Aaron when all Aaron was doing was holding up a mirror. He was just a conduit. Those melodies, stories, paintings, and colors belonged to the universe. That's why the captivation I drew from them didn't go away when he did.

By allowing Aaron to view my Instagram stories for nine years, I was keeping a portal open to his influence—a dormant connection that provided nothing of value. I picked up my phone from the nightstand, logged into my social accounts, and disconnected from him everywhere we were still connected. I did this not from bitterness, but out of respect for myself. I deserved *more* than whatever it was I was getting.

I set my phone down, relieved, and recalled the thing he'd said that'd kept me hostage for a decade, repeating the sentence aloud in the lamplight. "You will never meet anyone like me." The absurdity of the statement suddenly revealed itself. I laughed, cackled even, like a diabolical soothsayer on the edge of night. I extracted a single word from this line and separated it into two: *any one.* Then I wrote down all the qualities I prized in Aaron, qualities he insisted were so unique I might never find the combination in another: creativity, passion, tenderness, confidence, humor, cleverness, coolness.

I Googled *How many people are on the planet right now?* The answer: 7.853 billion.[57] If I were a betting girl, I'd put my money on *any one* of us summing these qualities. I knew this to be true because I was *one. I* was creative, passionate, tender, confident, funny, clever, and cool. We will all meet many *ones* in our lifetimes. We never need to change our sweatshirts, or the music we listen to, or how many cigarettes we do or don't smoke to be *one* or to know *one.* We only need to change the way we see.

• • •

My sisters ashes were bottled in a cream-colored urn, displayed on the living room mantle over a fake fireplace. A photograph of her smiling was propped next to it. I passed by

57 "Population: Current World Population," Worldometer, accessed March 19, 2021.

the urn every time I walked from my bedroom to the kitchen, which was about one hundred times a day. No matter how many times I saw the urn I never knew what to make of it, or how to process what was in there. I don't know yet if I ever will be able to. I am more patient now than I was when my sister first became ashes. I am willing to wait and see.

It took three years for the advice given to me after Allie's death, that I'd deemed as stupid or thoughtless, to feel not so stupid or thoughtless after all. Time had remarkably softened the impact of the hospital visuals I initially suspected would destroy me. Like flexing a muscle, the more I called upon happy memories of Allie, the more the bad faded away.

When I think of Allie now, I mostly hear her open-mouthed laugh—loud, a little scratchy, and as true as can be. I see her mannerisms, charm, and enthusiasm shining through my niece. Like the warmth of daybreak washing over my face, I feel her pulling me in for a noogie. I remembered how free I felt when we played "airplane"—when she laid on the carpet, jabbed her legs into the air, squeezed my hands with hers as I tilted forward on my abdomen. She held me aloft with her feet. I remember choreographing dances around a radio we set up in the garage. Doing jackknives and cannon balls into the pool, grading mighty splashes that sprinkled across the patio screen from the force of us.

• • •

Sometimes when we transform ourselves quickly, our people need time to catch up and adjust their expectations. Living in my childhood home with my family for the first time in over ten years inevitably grazed old wounds. However, the triggering ultimately brought us closer. Impromptu arguments or disagreements, over big topics like politics, or small topics like dirty dishes, were the "in the field" pop quizzes on everything I had been learning.

In all cases, I noticed I didn't hide or shade my needs. I couldn't even if I had wanted to. Confirmed: I had unlearned the technique. We didn't agree on everything that came up, but we were able to talk frankly and calmly about most things, even if there was a blowout that came first. Thus, we got to know each other all over again. We navigated the newness clumsily, but we had reparative conversations that were previously unimaginable.

I think of this transformation as a starling murmuration twisting through the sky. A hypnotic mass from afar, made up of individual creatures. When individual starlings change direction in a murmuration, it's called a "critical transition," which is also how I referred to my hardships. Each of my critical transitions taught me something about my values. Thanks to computer scientists, behavioral scientists, and theoretical physicists, we know through digital imaging that each starling in a murmuration takes behavioral cues from the closest seven starlings to it.[58] Like starlings, when we show up in the world as our most trusting, compassionate, and authentic selves, we encourage those around us to show up that way too.

• • •

I considered the extended time I was able to spend with my family a rare gift, but by the end of summer I missed having designated space to make art and privacy. My art supplies were toppling out of boxes, shoved in every corner. Though,

---

58 A. Jamie Wood, Colin Beale, "Ecology: Starling Murmurations: The Science Behind One of Nature's Greatest Displays," Phys.Org, February 6, 2019

I didn't want to go back to my small, dark apartment in DC either. I considered moving out of it even, but I was stressed by the liminal in-between. Neither place felt quite right. I wished someone would make the decision for me.

When the quarantine mandate was extended yet again through the winter, I decided to drive back to my DC apartment in late August and stay there just until the holidays. A childhood friend, Amy, who was also in Ormond for the summer, was heading north too, back to New York. We agreed to make the trip up together, but separately. She would drive up in her car and me in mine.

A feeling of foreshadowing occurred in the days leading up to our long-distance drive. I tried to ignore it as I packed up my things, but the anticipation was making me restless, giving me heart palpitations. My superpowers were loud and clear: *something is coming.*

After the first day's eight-hour stretch, we checked into a hotel overnight in Durham, North Carolina. The following morning, we crept downstairs in our pajamas to the continental breakfast, swiped some mini boxes of cereal, cartons of milk, and brought them back to our hotel room. We poured the cereal into Styrofoam bowls that we ate out of while lounging in our clean, white, hotel sheets. Amy asked me over the TV volume, crunching Fruit Loops between her teeth, "Hey, are you feeling alright? I noticed you were rolling around a lot in your sleep."

I looked over groggily at her in the bright, morning light slotting through the window curtains. "Yeah," I said, "I'm fine. I do feel anxious though. I'm not exactly sure why. I have a really weird feeling."

We checked out of the hotel and climbed into our separate cars, ready for the next eight-hour shift. Coasting down a state road at seventy miles per hour, I opened and closed my mouth, stretching my jaw. It was sore from hours of clenching my teeth. The closer we got to my apartment, my apprehension mounted. I didn't really smoke, but I pulled a CBD joint from a package that was gifted to me a month earlier from a shop owner I happened upon. I lit it, desperate to soothe my nerves. Smoke billowed dramatically from the end of the joint papers and filled the car.

Amy called my phone from her car, which was several minutes behind me. I was worried she'd caught up and seen the smoke streaming from my windows. Embarrassed, I jammed the joint into an empty soda can and swatted smoke away with my hand. She asked if she could crash overnight at my apartment once we got to DC and she'd continue on to New York in the morning. "Sure," I said. "I can make up the couch for you."

We pulled up to my apartment at 8:30 p.m. I parked in the driveway and helped Amy find parking for her car on Thirteenth Street. I threw open the front door and when we walked inside the house smelled funny. Musty. The air conditioning wall units were off, so I cranked them on full blast and slid open my small bedroom window to let in fresh air. Amy helped me unload my car, placing everything in a messy pile on the living room floor.

I dumped my purse on the bed and joined Amy who was relaxing on the couch in the living room. I sat down beside her and sneezed. I couldn't put my finger on why, but the house appeared inexplicably sullied, even though everything was tidied in its place like I'd left it three months earlier. We talked about grabbing something for dinner, but I needed to check to see what was open on a Sunday night. I stood up and walked into the bedroom to grab my phone off the bed.

When I reached out to pick it up, I noticed a hairy film over the surface of the comforter. It was green. Tripping backward, I glanced all around. The film was on everything: my clothing, my picture frames, my furniture, my jewelry. I screamed.

"Oh my God!" I shrieked.

"What!"

I ran back into the living room, breathless. "There's mold! It's everywhere!"

Both of our eyes shot to the couch where she sat. White spores deckled its seams.

• • •

While I was away, my landlord had turned off all of the wall AC units and never went downstairs to check on the apartment. There was no central AC and, as the humidity in DC summers is suffocating, the moisture inside of the apartment had bloomed an extravagant mold forest, covering everything. I was moving out, ASAP.

I stayed in a hotel room, which was my cheapest option due to Covid-19 surge pricing, for four days, processing. Luckily, my cousin and his wife who lived nearby offered to generously host me in their guest bedroom until I figured things out. During the first week of damage control, my landlord sent a sanitization crew to sterilize everything in my house. I was not allowed to touch any of my items before the sanitization, and I waited, mortified, as the team combed through everything I owned, including lingerie, lubricants, and other things.

Every waking minute of September, outside of my nine to five job, was spent cleaning. When I was finally allowed to go back into my unit, I purchased a hazmat suit, gloves, antimicrobial spray, and three sixty-four-ounce jugs of vinegar. I doused the clothing I determined might be salvageable, which was about six items out of one hundred, in repeated vinegar baths. I threw away furniture, clothing, camping supplies, backpacks, purses, rugs, cooking materials, cameras, camera straps, bedding, books, you name it.

Unexpectedly, as everything I owned drained from my possession, I began to feel a secret sense of relief.

• • •

There are select formats in which we prefer to honor or protect our most precious materials, like placing them inside of a frame, a safe, or a display case. A pile on the ground is not usually the preferred method, but it was all I could do. At night, I sat on the cold, tile floor and sifted through sealed plastic tubs that I'd dragged out from underneath my bed. Luckily, everything inside was dry and intact. They contained scrapbooks of old photos, notes, keepsakes, and diaries. Once all of my furniture was gone, like a fulcrum, I divided the things that felt irreplaceable into little piles in a ring around me, as if I was seated at the center of a crop circle. On their visits, mold inspectors stepped over and in between the floor piles, like landmines made of memories.

Reviewing the jumbled wreckage, the last thirty years flashed before me. In one pile was a mustard-colored ceramic dish that Allie had sculpted in elementary school. Her fingerprints were still pressed into the side. In another pile were projects from college, crinkled and held together by dried webs of hot glue—proof of my unyielding heart. I felt saddened for myself while reading the confused diary scribbles penned in my early twenties. I felt loved by the faded letters I'd saved from all of my ex-boyfriends. I cried tears of joy while leafing through thirty years of birthday cards, photographs, and postcards, brightened by the wealth of family and friendships I'd developed all over the globe.

Despite a legacy of feeling never prepared, not good enough, I combed the evidence of an already full, explorative life.

• • •

At the beginning of Covid-19, the nation had collectively contracted, financially and spiritually, in fear of layoffs and illness. I expressed in therapy "I'm so scared to lose my job. One of my worst fears is losing everything. What would I do? Where would I go?"

As mold spores ravaged my belongings, I was pushed to face my fear. And I'm not so sure everything *can* be lost. While dragging my mattress, box spring, and nightstand covered in mold through the back alley to the trash bins, I asked myself new questions. *Universe,* I posed, sweat dripping from my temples, *what am I supposed to be learning from all of this? I know there must be a lesson here. What is this supposed to be teaching me?*

Like the miscellany of dew dappled over morning branches, disks of lichen studding the trunks of trees, and matted, decomposing leaves, the answer to this question was in my trash can overflowing with dirty paper towels. It was in the hair pins, books, yoga mats, and dusty picture frames strewn around my apartment floor. Beneath this surface pandemonium was order and unseen purpose. With every passing day, I increasingly struggled to label the mold growth, and resulting evacuation, as "good" or "bad" because it is impossible to know what place or purpose a seemingly random event has within the tapestry of our lives.[59]

---

59 Eckhart Tolle, *A New Earth: Awakening to Your Life's Purpose* (New York: Viking Press, 2005) 196–197.

The mold was a G.I. Joe, asking "You ready for this?" and bashing a hole in my life with the front wheel of a roller-blade. Doubly, I found I was not unmoored as I had previously been in the event of disaster. My resilience had already proven to me I was disaster proof. I knew I no longer needed to panic or abandon myself to pull through.

On the final day of September 2020, I dropped my house key through my landlord's mail slot. Important documents, photographs, and keepsakes were packed into a small storage unit down the street. The little else that remained of my possessions were piled so high in the front and back seats of my car that I couldn't see out the windows or behind me.

Heading to my cousin's cabin in West Virginia for a few days to draft a plan, I merged onto the interstate. I sped past truck drivers that ogled from above, seeing me in all my nakedness—me and my few belongings—baptisms of new beginnings. My curly hair whipped around my face in the wind like a lion's mane or a decorative wreath. I didn't know where I would land next, but I contained something lossless and invaluable within myself: trust.

Iridescent, I flew through the hole in the drywall, up the stairs, and out the back door.

ACKNOWLEDGMENTS

I could write a second book on all I've learned through publishing this one. The talented individuals I had the privilege of working with taught me how to speak up, ask for help, and stand proudly in my worth. I will carry this through the rest of my life.

I'd like to thank New Degree Press founder, Eric Koester, for including me in his program and fulfilling his early promise to purchase a copy of my book. I'd like to thank author and coach, Haley Newlin, for encouraging me to drag Trich out of my shadow and into the light. I'd like to thank my developmental editor, Karina L. Agbisit, for combing my enormous first draft, and for asking good, thoughtful, and expansive questions. I'd like to thank my marketing and revisions editor, Kendra Kadam, for being a bastion of positivity and stability through the challenging stage of revisions. I'd like to thank head of publishing, Brian Bies, for his resourcefulness, encouragement, and availability. I'd like to acknowledge every other person who assisted in the making of this book who is not individually mentioned, including my cover designers, citation gurus, layout editors, and copy editors. Thank you to my Beta readers, Julie G., Julie P., Lizzie, Kallie, Katelyn,

Kayla Mae, and Natalie for your time, honesty, and smarts. I'd like to thank my cohort for their insight and camaraderie.

I have enormous gratitude for my Mom, who has moved me with her willingness to have challenging conservations, often until wee hours of the morning. Mom, thank you for your vulnerability, love, and support in every way. Thank you to Kevin and Cayden for letting me space invade throughout 2020 to 2021. For laughing with and at me, while I've worked day and night. Thank you to Pete and Sarah for putting me up in your rural paradise at the beginning of this project when my house was falling apart. Thank you to all of my relatives who have supported me near and far, financially, emotionally, or otherwise. I see you and appreciate you.

(In alphabetical order) Thank you Evelyn for your depth, laughter, adventure, and for letting me look out at the world by your side. Thank you to Kallie for your warmth, wisdom, and soulful ambiance. Thank you to Julie P. for your thoughtfulness, kindness, and quarantine check-ins. Thank you to Katelyn for deleting all of my voicemails that one day when I could not. For your sparkle, spontaneity, and being the best hype woman I could ask for. Thank you to Kayla Mae for your lifelong companionship. For your silliness and strength; a lighthouse from your bike to your bathtub. Thank you to Lizzy for a decade of advice, intimacy, and humor, uniquely traversing the audio waves. Sister eyes, sister lives. Thank you forever to Megan and Robert for lending me your car and your support when I needed it the most. Thank you to Natalie for pre-reading a substantial portion of my book, your honesty and heart, and our revelatory therapy sessions tangled with creative vision. I'd like to thank Sika's beautiful spirit for introducing me to all things healing. Thank you to *all* my DC friends, especially my coven, Ellie, Julie S.,

Lauren, and Lizzie, for your individuality, comedic genius, and emotional support.

A special thank you to every single person mentioned in this book, directly or indirectly, for helping shape my life; for teaching me something valuable, regardless of context. Thank you to my high school and college friends, especially Alex, Emily, Holly, Jamie, Meagan, Megan, and Molly, whose love and generosity suspends time and distance. Our continued relationships bring me joy and belonging. I could write a thousand stories about us and none of them would fit into my word count. I'd like to thank Dr. Markisha Bennett for her grace and expertise, and for sticking by me through and through.

A special thank you to every person who believed I had something worth saying by supporting my campaign:

Alanna Vanacore

Alex Doan

Alex Prokop

Alison Szopinski

Amanda Allen

Amanda Almaguer

Amy Doyel

Amy Morse

Amy Stevens

Anais Vaval

Andrew Barry

Andy Wyatt

Anna Williams

Anthony W. Orrach

April Musser

Ashley Parkins

Bailey Whisler

Blake Coglianese

Bradley J. Freed

Bridget Bradley

Carol King Woodward

Carol Volante

Carrie Spilfogel

Cecilia Cortes-Earle

Chad Smith

Charles M. Avena

Chrissy Mccrimmon

Christine Ostrosky

Coleen Flanagan

Cyril Rodriguez

Danielle Carrico

Dany Green

Darlene Teracino

David Paul Johnson

Deb Knapp

Donna Flanagan

Donna Staton

Elizabeth Zack

Elnoosh Ghazizadeh

Emily Covell

Emily Kelly

Emily Townsend-Cobb

Emily Whelan

Eric Koester

Eric Quintanilla

Erik Smith

Evelyn Rhodes

Holly O'Hearn

J. Oliver Schak

Jaimee Perritt

Jake New

Jamie Sanchez

Jeff Paccione

Jennifer Liebschutz

Jesse Sison

Jim Van Meer

Joe Taravella

Jonathan Farley

Josephine Mitchell

Josh Lasky

Julianna Gram

Julianne Soluri

Julie Paulson

Julie Sheah

Kaitlyn Frey

Kallie Martin

Karen Avena

Katelyn Chapel

Kathy Hart
Kayla Mae Davis
Kelly Grosskurth
Kelly Kelly
Kim Vo
Kimi Alfonzo
Kriselle Fitzgerald
Kristen Kruger
Laura Bissonnette
Laura McHugh
Lauren Coughlin
Lauren Puglisi
Leo Brussel
Linda Flanagan
Lizzie White
Luis Perez
Mariah Fox
Mary Owens
Matthew Merolli
Maureen Flanary
Meagan Blake
Meagan Silva
Megan Larmie
Michael Lee
Michelle Dozier
Michelle Howard
Mollie Ruskin
Molly Larmie
Morgan Bailie
Morgan Reeves
Natalie Ivis
Nicola Avena
Nicole James
Patrice Auletta
Patti Debow
Payam Ostovar
Phoebe O'Dell
Raleigh Davis
Regan Anderson
Richard Paccione
Rick Sasiain
Ryan Cobb
Sam Feigenbaum
Sam Tranfa
Samantha Trattler
Sara Costa

Sarah Davis
Shane Galley
Shannon Cullen
Shannon Healy
Steven Odermatt
Susan Greco
Tasha Yost
Tom Kim
Tyler Martin
Umair Ahsan
Vaughn McDonald
Victoria Thompson
Vincent Sylvester
William Bradford Smith
Xena Ni
Yohanka Munoz

I am so very lucky for you.

APPENDIX

AUTHORS NOTE

Online Etymology Dictionary. Douglas Harper, 2001–2021. Accessed January 29, 2021. https://www.etymonline.com/word/victim#:~:text=victim%20(n.),a%20word%20of%20uncertain%20origin.

CHAPTER 1

Beyond Words. "Why Badmouthing the Other Parent Hurts Your Child." Accessed January 7, 2021. https://www.growbeyondwords.com/why-badmouthing-the-other-parent-hurts-your-child/#:~:text=It%20can%20lead%20to%20poor,between%20his%20or%20her%20parents.

Graham, Chris. "Daytona Beach Not the Spring Break Hot Spot It Once Was." *The Daytona Beach News-Journal.* March 23, 2013. https://www.news-journalonline.com/article/LK/20130323/News/605062725/DN.

Massey, Alexandra. "What Are the Dysfunctional Family Archetypal Rules and Roles?" *AlexandraMassey.co.uk* (blog). Updated June 10, 2020. http://www.chronicle.com/blogs/linguafranca/2017/02/15/futurist-shock/.

On Call International (blog). "The History of Spring Break Travel: A Retrospective." March 7, 2013. Accessed January 8, 2021. https://blog.oncallinternational.com/the-history-of-spring-break-travel-a-retrospective/#:~:text=1990's%E2%80%94%20The%20Daytona%20spring%20break,the%20sun%20is%20even%20hotter.

Tolle, Eckhart. *A New Earth: Awakening to Your Life's Purpose.* New York: Viking Press, 2005.

CHAPTER 2

Statista. "Number of Children Living with a Single Mother or a Single Father in the US from 1970 to 2019." Demographics. Last modified November 2019. https://www.statista.com/statistics/252847/number-of-children-living-with-a-single-mother-or-single-father/.

CHAPTER 3

Homeland Security Digital Library. "Timeline: Aviation and Transportation Security Act." Accessed January 9, 2021. https://www.hsdl.org/c/tl/aviation-transportation-security-act/.

Witte, G. "Afghanistan War." Encyclopedia Britannica, October 31, 2020. https://www.britannica.com/event/Afghanistan-War.

CHAPTER 4

Amish America. "What Is the Amish Ordnung?" Accessed January 16, 2021. https://amishamerica.com/what-is-the-amish-ordnung/.

Shipshewana Indiana. "Visit Shipshewana Indiana." Accessed January 16, 2021. https://www.shipshewana.com/.

Shipshewana Trading Place. "Vendor Directory." Accessed January 16, 2021. https://shipshewanatradingplace.com/flea-market/vendor-directory/.

The National Child Traumatic Stress Network. "Complex Trauma: Effects." Accessed January 10, 2021. https://www.nctsn.org/what-is-child-trauma/trauma-types/complex-trauma/effects.

Van Der Kolk, Bessel. *The Body Keeps the Score: Brain, Mind, and Body in the Healing of Trauma.* New York: Penguin Books, 2015.

CHAPTER 5

Forbes. "Forbes Lists." Accessed February 15, 2021. https://www.forbes.com/lists/list-directory/#5fc34aeb274d.

Smith, Lauren. "How the Spice Girls Really Got Their Names." Gazia. September 09, 2015. https://graziadaily.co.uk/celebrity/news/spice-girls-got-names-mel-b-peter-loraine/.

CHAPTER 6

Ancient History Encyclopedia. s.v. "Romulus and Remus." By Brittany Garcia. Published April, 18, 2018. https://www.ancient.eu/Romulus_and_Remus/.

Guttmacher Institute. "Adolescent Sexual and Reproductive Health in the United States." Sexual Intercourse Among Young People in the US Figure 1. Updated September 2019. https://www.guttmacher.org/fact-sheet/american-teens-sexual-and-reproductive-health.

CHAPTER 7

National Institute on Alcohol Abuse and Alcoholism. "Alcohol's Effects on Health: College Drinking." Updated January 2021. https://www.niaaa.nih.gov/publications/brochures-and-fact-sheets/college-drinking.

CHAPTER 8

Chamberlain, Samuel R., Michael Harries, Sarah A. Redden, et al. "Cortical Thickness Abnormalities in Trichotillomania: International Multi-Site Analysis." *Brain Imaging and Behavior* 12. (June 2017): 823–828 https://doi.org/10.1007/s11682-017-9746-3.

CHAPTER 9

Marich, Jamie. "Reptilian Brain of Survival and Mammalian Brain." Gracepoint. Accessed February 20, 2021. https://www.gracepointwellness.org/109-post-traumatic-stress-disorder/article/55760-reptilian-brain-of-survival-and-mammalian-brain.

Muller, Robert T. "Trauma Survivors at Risk for Future Abusive Relationships." *Psychology Today*, January 8, 2016. https://www.psychologytoday.com/us/blog/talking-about-trauma/201601/trauma-survivors-risk-future-abusive-relationships.

Office for National Statistics. "Crime and Justice: People Who Were Abused as Children Are More Likely to Be Abused as an Adult." September 7, 2017. https://www.ons.gov.uk/peoplepopulationandcommunity/crimeandjustice/articles/peoplewhowereabusedaschildrenaremorelikelytobeabusedasanadult/2017-09 27#:~:text=More%20than%20half%20(57%25),26%25%20compared%20with%20 14%25.

Van Der Kolk, Bessel. *The Body Keeps the Score: Brain, Mind, and Body in the Healing of Trauma*. New York: Penguin Books, 2015.

CHAPTER 10

Greece.com. "Info: Greek Cross." Accessed January 23, 2021. https://www.greece.com/info/general/greek_cross/.

Stanford Encyclopedia of Philosophy. s.v. "Pythagoreanism." Substantive revision July 31, 2019. https://plato.stanford.edu/entries/pythagoreanism/#:~:text=(1)%20 Pythagoreanism%20is%20the%20philosophy,body%2C%20human%20or%20animal.

Uliano, Dick. "DC Tops List of Nation's Worst Traffic Gridlock." *WtopNews*, August 26, 2017. https://www.nytimes.com/2017/03/08/technology/snap-makes-a-bet-on-the-cultural-supremacy-of-the-camera.html.

CHAPTER 11

Atasoy, Ozgun. "Your Thoughts Can Release Abilities Beyond Normal Limits." *Scientific American*, August 13, 2013. https://www.scientificamerican.com/article/your-thoughts-can-release-abilities-beyond-normal-limits/.

CHAPTER 14

McDougall, Christopher. *Born to Run: A Hidden Tribe, Superathletes, and the Greatest Race the World Has Never Seen.* New York: Vintage, 2011.

Tolle, Eckhart. *A New Earth: Awakening to Your Life's Purpose.* New York: Viking Press, 2005.

Van Der Kolk, Bessel. *The Body Keeps the Score: Brain, Mind, and Body in the Healing of Trauma.* New York: Penguin Books, 2015.

CHAPTER 15

Rodenburg, Malissa, "From Memory to Motor Skills, Running Improves Brain Function." Women's Running. July 2, 2020. https://www.womensrunning.com/health/running-improves-brain-function/#:~:text=While%20the%20immediate%20benefit%20of,lasting%20changes%20to%20brain%20function.

Wisniewski, Allie. "Nurse Logs: Healers of the Forest." *American Forests* (blog). *The Official Blog of American Forests,* July 12, 2017. https://www.americanforests.org/blog/nurse-logs-healers-forest/.

CHAPTER 16

Kuhn, Robert Lawrence. "Confronting the Multiverse: What 'Infinite Universes' Would Mean." Space.com. December 23, 2015. https://www.space.com/31465-is-our-universe-just-one-of-many-in-a-multiverse.html.

CHAPTER 17

National Park Service. "Sand Dunes: Geology." Accessed March 4, 2021. https://www.nps.gov/grsa/learn/nature/sanddunes.htm#:~:text=Scientists%20don't%20yet%20know,)%2C%20is%20still%20in%20development.

Zimmermann, Susan. *Writing to Heal the Soul: Transforming Grief and Loss Through Writing.* New York: The Crown Publishing Group, 2002.

CHAPTER 18

Van Der Kolk, Bessel. *The Body Keeps the Score: Brain, Mind, and Body in the Healing of Trauma.* New York: Penguin Books, 2015.

Westover, Tara. *Educated.* New York City: Penguin Random House LLC., 2018.

CHAPTER 19

Kriegsman, Alan M. "Dance." *Washington Post,* March 29, 1989. https://www.washingtonpost.com/archive/lifestyle/1989/03/29/dance/ea0862e7-6d28-4f8f-899b-3c86e9efbc8c/.

CHAPTER 20

Brown, Brené. *Daring Greatly: How the Courage to Be Vulnerable Transforms the Way We Live, Love, Parent, and Lead.* New York: Avery, 2015.

"Learn the Lingo: Manifestation Glossary." To Be Magnetic. Accessed March 18, 2021. https://tobemagnetic.com/qa-index-library.

Pflanzer, Lydia Ramsey and Samantha Lee. "Our DNA Is 99.9% the Same as the Person Next to Us." Business Insider. Accessed March 18, 2019. https://www.businessinsider.com/comparing-genetic-similarity-between-humans-and-other-things-2016-5.

"Q/A Index Library: Unblocked Shadow." To Be Magnetic. Accessed March 18, 2021. https://tobemagnetic.com/qa-index-library.

To Be Magnetic. "Free Exercise: Get Clarity." Accessed March 18, 2021. https://to-be-magnetic-manifestation-school.teachablecom/p/free-exercise-get-clarity.

CHAPTER 21

Paulson, Steve. "Your Brain Makes You a Different Person Every Day." *Nautilus,* October 14, 2020. https://nautil.us/issue/91/the-amazing-brain/your-brain-makes-you-a-different-person-every-day.

"Population: Current World Population." Worldometer. Accessed March 19, 2021. https://tobemagnetic.com/qa-index-library.

Tolle, Eckhart. *A New Earth: Awakening to Your Life's Purpose.* New York: Viking Press, 2005.

Wood, Jamie and Colin Beale. "Ecology: Starling Murmurations: The Science Behind One of Nature's Greatest Displays." Phys.Org. February 6, 2019.

CPSIA information can be obtained
at www.ICGtesting.com
Printed in the USA
JSHW030333170521
14734JS00002B/5